KANGAROO PAWS
AND

A NATURAL HISTORY AND FIELD GUIDE

Stephen D. Hopper
Principal Photographers
Babs and Bert Wells

Published by:
Dr Syd Shea, Executive Director,
Department of Conservation and Land Management,
50 Hayman Road, Como, Western Australia 6152

Executive Editor:
Ron Kawalilak

Managing Editor:
Ray Bailey

Editor:
Kate Hooper

Design:
Stacey Strickland

Printed in Western Australia by:
Scott Four Colour

Cartography:
CALM Land information Branch

Illustrations:
Margaret Pieroni

Cover photography:
Common green kangaroo paw
Anigozanthos viridis subsp. *viridis* (Babs and Bert Wells)

© Copyright CALM 1993. ISBN 9 780730 959137
All material in this book is copyright and may not be reproduced except with the written permission of the publishers.

 Department of Conservation and Land Management
Perth, Western Australia 1993

3039 0693 5M

To Patricia, Donald and Christine Hopper

for their inspiration,

and to Luke, Jonathan and Claire

for the future

PREFACE

South-western Australia offers the wildflower enthusiast unparalleled opportunities to explore and discover, with an estimated 8 000 species of plants, three-quarters of which are found nowhere else, and about a third of which are still to be officially described.

The kangaroo paws and catspaws are the south-western flora in microcosm. There are 12 species of breathtaking colour and shape, several of them closely related; some are the result of explosive evolution over the climatically turbulent past two million years. How do you identify the species? How have so many evolved in the south-west? Why are their flowers so strikingly coloured? Are any of them endangered, and if so, how might they be best conserved for the future? How have they reached the vanguard of the horticultural development of Australian native flora?

The aim of this book is to explore these questions. Believing that the first step in conservation is recognition, I hope that the book will help to stimulate awareness and appreciation of the wonderful wildflowers of the south-west.

The idea for collaborative work on this book arose in discussions with Babs and Bert Wells in July 1981. It grew out of our mutual interest in the natural history of a special group of plants in a very special part of the world.

Many people assisted in the preparation of the book. First and foremost, I am indebted to Babs and Bert Wells for their help, friendship and patience. In addition to their superb photographic contribution, Bert put together the initial draft of Chapter 13. Dr Sid James, with other members of the Department of Botany at the University of Western Australia, guided and supported the author through five fascinating years of postgraduate research on the kangaroo paws. Keith Oliver (now at Murdoch University) and Bob Dixon (Kings Park and Botanic Garden), both masters of kangaroo paw horticulture, provided encouragement over the past two decades. Both offered useful comments on the manuscript, as did Dr Neville Marchant (Western Australian Herbarium) and Dr Kingsley Dixon (Kings Park and Botanic Garden). Staff at various herbaria have materially assisted my research. I am grateful to many other colleagues, too numerous to name, who freely provided information. USA botanists Professor Bob Ornduff (University of California, Berkeley), Dr Al Gentry (Missouri Botanical Garden) and Professor Robert Wyatt (University of Georgia) provided or helped gather colour slides of African and American Haemodoraceae. The necessary executive backing was given by Ron Kawalilak, while editorial support was expertly provided by Dr Kate Hooper and Dr Ray Bailey. Margaret Pieroni provided the delightful drawings, and Stacey Strickland, design. And lastly, my extended family members deserve heartfelt thanks for their support.

CONTENTS

1. INTRODUCTION 9
2. RELATIONSHIPS BETWEEN PLANTS 11
3. THE UNIQUE KANGAROO PAWS 19
4. WHERE TO FIND KANGAROO PAWS 25
5. SEEDERS AND SPROUTERS 29
6. POLLINATION 33
7. POLLEN AND NECTAR POACHERS 43
8. MIXED MARRIAGES: NATURAL HYBRIDISATION 49
9. A FAMILY HISTORY 55
10. PIONEERING BOTANISTS 65
11. A GROWING REPUTATION 81
12. BIODIVERSITY: THE KEY TO OUR FUTURE 89

GLOSSARY 96

FIELD GUIDE: LEARNING TO RECOGNISE KANGAROO PAWS 101
    How to use this Field Guide 101
1. Red kangaroo paw *Anigozanthos rufus* 103
2. Yellow kangaroo paw *Anigozanthos pulcherrimus* 105
3. Evergreen kangaroo paw *Anigozanthos flavidus* 106
4. Albany catspaw *Anigozanthos preissii* 108
5. Branched catspaw *Anigozanthos onycis* 111
6. Catspaw *Anigozanthos humilis* 113
6a. Common catspaw *Anigozanthos humilis* subsp. *humilis* 113
6b. Mogumber catspaw *Anigozanthos humilis* subsp. *chrysanthus* 114
6c. Giant catspaw *Anigozanthos humilis* subsp. 'grandis' 117
7. Kalbarri catspaw *Anigozanthos kalbarriensis* 118
8. Dwarf kangaroo paw *Anigozanthos gabrieliae* 120
9. Two-coloured kangaroo paw *Anigozanthos bicolor* 122
9a. Two-coloured kangaroo paw *Anigozanthos bicolor* subsp. *bicolor* 122
9b. Long-flowered kangaroo paw *Anigozanthos bicolor* subsp. *exstans* 124
9c. Forest kangaroo paw *Anigozanthos bicolor* subsp. *decrescens* 126
9d. Little kangaroo paw *Anigozanthos bicolor* subsp. *minor* 129
10. Green kangaroo paw *Anigozanthos viridis* 131
10a. Common green kangaroo paw *Anigozanthos viridis* subsp. *viridis* 131
10b. Dwarf green kangaroo paw *Anigozanthos viridis* subsp. *terraspectans* 132
10c. Metallic green kangaroo paw *Anigozanthos viridis* subsp. 'metallica' 134
11. Red and green kangaroo paw *Anigozanthos manglesii* 137
11a. Mangles' kangaroo paw *Anigozanthos manglesii* subsp. *manglesii* 137
11b. Northern red and green kangaroo paw *Anigozanthos manglesii* subsp. *quadrans* 138
12. Black kangaroo paw *Macropidia fuliginosa* 140

Index 144

The Coat of Arms of the State of Western Australia

The red and green kangaroo paw (*Anigozanthos manglesii*) has become a cultural symbol of Western Australia since its selection in 1960 as the State Floral Emblem. Here, two flower heads flank the royal crown on the coat of arms of Western Australia, which was granted by Her Majesty Queen Elizabeth II by Royal Warrant on 17 March 1969. The kangaroo paws join two male red kangaroos and the black swan to represent the unique flora and characteristic fauna of Western Australia.

Introduction

There are few groups of plants recognised as so typically Australian as the kangaroo paws and catspaws. Their striking floral colours and attractiveness as garden plants and cut flowers place the kangaroo paws alongside eucalypts, wattles, wax flowers and banksias in terms of their international appeal. Yet there are many features of these popular flowers that are not well known. Even the fact that there are 12 species, not just the one red and green kangaroo paw, and that all 12 are found in the wild only in south-western Australia, comes as a surprise to many people.

This book aims to illustrate all the kangaroo paw species and subspecies, and provide information to help, not just with identification, but with understanding.

In many ways, the kangaroo paws have been in the forefront of developments in Australian horticulture and biological research. They were among the first native plants to be experimentally hybridised in the quest for superior cultivars, and they are now extensively propagated through commercial tissue culture.

In biological research, the kangaroo paws have proved to be excellent experimental subjects for unravelling the origins of the remarkable richness of the south-west Australian flora. They have also been important in studies of pollination by birds, and of the process of natural hybridisation. Their lives exemplify strategies that enable native plants to cope with fire.

In the cut-flower trade, the kangaroo paws have become truly international ambassadors of the Australian flora. They are exported fresh or dried all over the world, being especially popular in western Europe and Japan. And at home, the massed bushland displays of kangaroo paws are part of the rich floral wealth appreciated by tourists and locals alike in the south-west each spring.

The popular appeal of the kangaroo paws was demonstrated by the selection, in 1960, of the red and green kangaroo paw (*Anigozanthos manglesii*) as the State Floral Emblem of Western Australia. This species has been used on trademarks, coats of arms and letterheads by numerous Western Australian organisations and businesses.

The way in which the kangaroo paws have been adopted and accepted by so many Australians as beautiful and valued parts of our natural heritage, bodes well for their future. Perhaps the kangaroo paws will instil greater appreciation of native plants in general, and heighten concern for the conservation of a truly remarkable biological resource: the south-west Australian flora.

The two kangaroo paw genera

The *Anigozanthos* genus includes 11 species, whereas the genus *Macropidia* includes only one species, *Macropidia fuliginosa*, the black kangaroo paw. The two kangaroo paw genera are readily distinguished by means of their flowers. *Macropidia* has black and green flowers that are divided into six recurved lobes halfway up. The pollen-bearing stamens are projected outwards in an arch 25–35 mm long. There is only one ovule in each of the three chambers of the swollen ovary at the base of each flower. When the fertilised ovules ripen into seeds, each seed falls away with the outer ovary wall still attached. *Macropidia* is also distinct from the *Anigozanthos* species ecologically, being the only kangaroo paw that grows in brown gravelly conglomerate, rather than sand or sandy loam. By contrast, plants of the *Anigozanthos* genus have flowers that are green, red and green, reddish yellow, orange, or red. They are split into lobes only in the terminal quarter, and the stamens project outwards no more than 15 mm. Each chamber of the ovary contains two or more ovules, and ripe seeds are shed from splits along the top of the ovary in most species. Seeds of *Anigozanthos* are dramatically smaller than those of *Macropidia* (see page 19). Despite concerted efforts, no hybrid has ever been produced between *Macropidia* and *Anigozanthos*, whereas all species within the *Anigozanthos* genus will yield hybrids (some very rarely) when cross-pollinated.

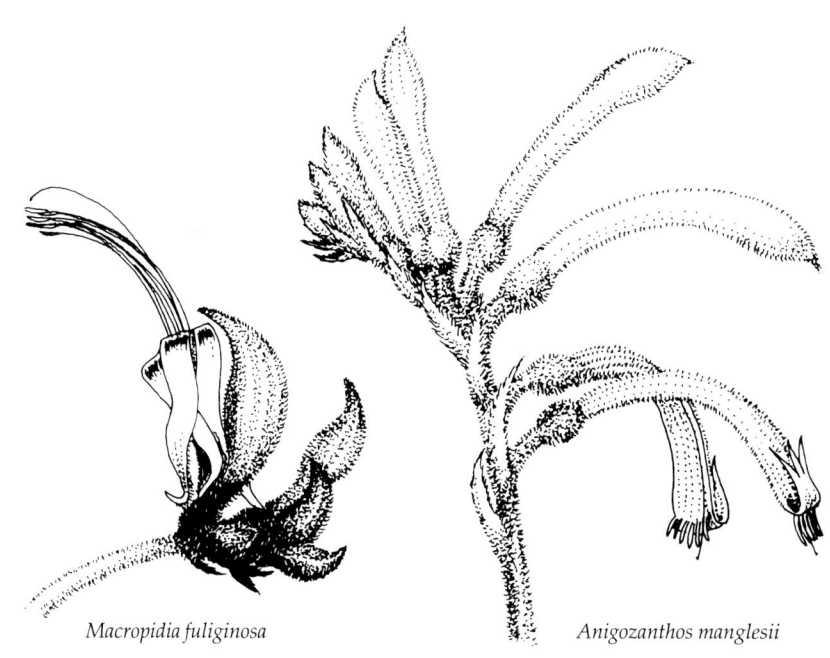

Macropidia fuliginosa   *Anigozanthos manglesii*

Relationships between plants

The botanical names that we use for different plant species are both a reliable way of referring to species, and a useful indicator of the relationships between plants. The kangaroo paws have their closest relatives in south-western Australia, but belong to a family extending from Australia to South Africa and the Americas.

A species is often defined as a group of organisms that share certain distinguishing features not found in other such groups. For example, all individuals of the yellow kangaroo paw species *Anigozanthos pulcherrimus* have yellow flowers and leaves 5–15 mm wide, whereas those of the closely related but distinct species the red kangaroo paw (*A. rufus*) have red flowers and leaves 2–6 mm wide.

Species may also be defined by their breeding relationships. Pollination between individuals of the same species produces offspring that are fully fertile, but cross-pollination between different species may result in hybrid progeny that are less fertile. If you cross-pollinate individuals of the red and green kangaroo paw *A. manglesii* from the same wild population and germinate the resultant seed, 97% of the pollen in the offspring will be normal in shape and fully functional. In contrast, if you hybridise *A. manglesii* with the common catspaw *A. humilis* and germinate the hybrid seed, only 25% of the pollen in the resulting hybrid flowers will be normal and functional. Such a test affirms that *A. manglesii* and *A. humilis* are distinct species.

When a group of species have features in common, they are usually presumed to share a common ancestor. Such an evolutionarily related group is called a genus. For example, all gum trees belong in the genus *Eucalyptus*, and all the kangaroo paws are placed in the genera *Anigozanthos* and *Macropidia*.

Using botanical names

The combination of generic and specific Latin names (called a binomial) result in a unique botanical name for all species of plants. During the early stages of classification there may be some changes to the botanical name of a plant if botanists disagree on the genus in which a species is placed, or regard species as varieties or subspecies, or discover an earlier name for a species. They may also discover on careful study that a 'variable' species actually comprises several similar-looking species. However, once such matters have been resolved, and for many named species this is the case, the Latin binomial is a stable and unique identifier.

The advantage of a binomial is that there is no danger of confusing the different species. This is not always the case with common names. For example, in the past *Anigozanthos manglesii* has been variously referred to as *kurulbrang, kuttych,* the kangaroo paw, the red and green kangaroo paw, the common kangaroo paw, or Mangles' kangaroo paw. For this reason, botanists tend to use the Latin binomials when communicating.

However, in the case of the kangaroo paws, most of the common names are descriptive, well known and informative. Therefore, both the common name and the scientific binomial of kangaroo paw species have been used throughout the book, as appropriate (see the index for a list).

Often, distinct races of a species are seen in different parts of its geographical range. In such circumstances, botanists may name subspecies. These are referred to after the abbreviation 'subsp.' or 'ssp.' following a species name. For example, the distinctive golden yellow race of *A. humilis* from Mogumber

Kangaroo paws and catspaws

The name 'kangaroo paw' (originally 'kangaroo foot') was coined in about the 1850s, and used mainly for *A. manglesii*, the red and green kangaroo paw common around Perth. Subsequently, its use has been extended to all the taller species, and those smaller species and subspecies that are red and green, or green (for example, *A. gabrieliae, A. viridis* subsp. *terrespectans*). The origin of the name 'catspaw' has not been traced, but it is likely to have been coined to contrast the small scapes and flowers of *A. humilis* with the tall, robust red and green kangaroo paw. There are now four species that are called by the common name catspaw: *A. humilis, A. kalbarriensis, A. onycis* and *A. preissii*. They have orange, reddish-orange, or yellow flowers, and usually have short scapes. In most catspaws the perianth lobes are thrust forwards rather than recurved.

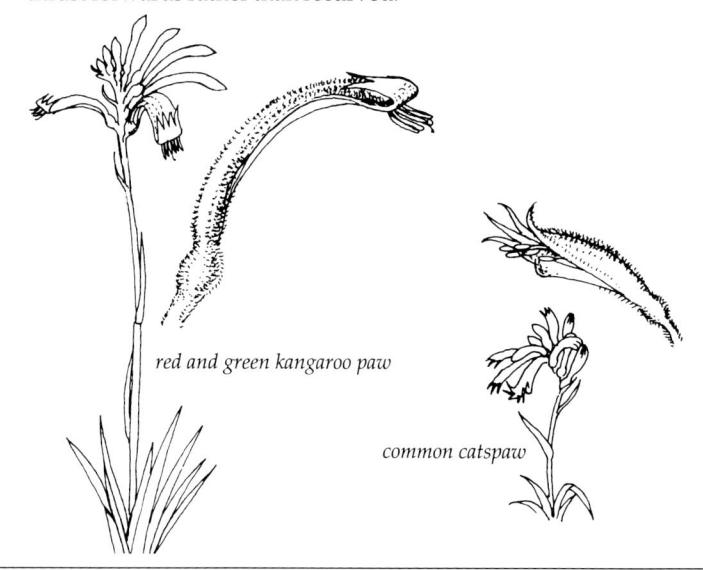

red and green kangaroo paw

common catspaw

is known as *A. humilis* subsp. *chrysanthus*, whereas the common catspaw race is *A. humilis* subsp. *humilis*.

The concept of subspecies is tending to replace an earlier category, 'variety' (abbreviated to 'var.'), which was widely used for recognisably different forms of species, irrespective of their geographical distribution. In some cases, named varieties were the same as modern subspecies; in others they were merely unusual forms found growing with normal individuals. For example, a rare yellow form of *A. manglesii* occasionally found in normal red and green populations was named *A. manglesii* var. *flavescens*. In other cases, named varieties have turned out to be distinct species in their own right. This conflicting usage of 'variety' has gradually led to its abandonment in favour of the more precisely defined subspecies concept.

Natural hybrids derived from cross-pollination of distinct species are usually referred to by a formula comprising the names of the two parental species linked by an 'x'. For example, *Anigozanthos manglesii x viridis* is the name given to the offspring resulting from cross-pollination between red and green kangaroo paws and green kangaroo paws. In the nursery trade, however, many hybrids are given cultivar (cultivated variety) names rather than hybrid formulae. For example, *Anigozanthos* 'Dwarf Delight' is a synthesised hybrid of *A. flavidus* and *A. onycis*.

Family resemblances

We use the fact that species share similar features to group them within a particular genus. If we can find basic features that are common to several genera, we can group these genera together into a family. For example, eucalypts are placed in the family Myrtaceae, along with melaleucas, bottlebrushes, wax-flowers, lilli-pillis, guavas and the Mediterranean myrtles from which the family name is derived. They all have glands in their leaves containing aromatic oils, which are responsible for one of the characteristic aromas of the Australian bush. Looking at the similarities and differences between genera in a family group can provide clues as to the evolutionary relationships between them.

The two kangaroo paw genera, *Anigozanthos* and *Macropidia*, are placed in the family Haemodoraceae. (The word comes from *haima* meaning 'blood', and *doron* meaning 'gift', alluding to the red colouring of the whole plant of some tropical species in the family.)

The Haemodoraceae (including the bloodroots, kangaroo paws, and cottonheads or coneflowers) is an old, and predominantly southern hemisphere, family of 14 genera and 103 species. All members have unusual chemicals, the arylphenalenones (one of which is named haemocorin), which cause the reddish-orange colour in the root structures of many species. These chemicals are not known elsewhere in the plant kingdom. They were used as a dye by Aboriginal Australians and by native North Americans from what is now the south-east United States. Haemocorin also shows promise as a pharmaceutical, having both antitumour and antibacterial activity.

Conostylis (coneflowers), with 46 species, is the largest genus of the Haemodoraceae. It, together with the genera *Anigozanthos* (11 species), *Macropidia* (one), *Blancoa* (one), *Tribonanthes* (five) and *Phlebocarya* (three), are all confined to south-western Australia (see page 98).

The genus *Haemodorum* (20 species), after which the family is named, is more widely distributed in Australia, with one species extending into New Guinea. It was a genus of considerable importance to Aboriginal Australians. The scarlet corms of the species *H. spicatum* are known by the Nyungars of south-western Australia as *mean* (*meen* or *meerne*), or *bohn*. They were often roasted and pounded to provide a paste of "acrid and unpleasant taste" like "a very mild onion" to the European colonial palate. This was such a staple in the Albany district that the local Aborigines referred to themselves as the *Meanager* (those who eat *mean*).

There are other genera of the family Haemodoraceae distributed across South Africa and the Americas. It is probable that the family arose when Australia, Antarctica, South America and Africa were all connected some 80 million years ago, as part of the great southern continent Gondwana. Progressive rifting eventually caused Gondwana to break up into the continents that we know today (see page 17), and the animal and plant groups that were spread across Gondwana became isolated from one another. In the course of time, they all evolved independently in their new continents and became less and less alike. Now, the few features that unite the members of a family such as the Haemodoraceae (their unique haemocorin), which is spread across the globe, are all that remain to tell us that they once had a common ancestor.

Interestingly, one of the two major groups or subfamilies recognised within the Haemodoraceae, the subfamily Conostylidoideae, comprises the six genera mentioned above that are found only in south-western Australia, and that include the kangaroo paws. This confinement suggests that a very long period of independent evolution has occurred in the south-west of Western Australia. There is little doubt that members of this part of the family are related to each other and share a common origin, probably in the south-west, but botanists have found relationships among the other members of the Haemodoraceae more difficult to resolve.

Exactly who is related to who among the American and African Haemodoraceae is not entirely clear, and will require careful future study. What does seem clear, however, is that the American, African and tropical Australian members of the family have features likely to be more similar to the tropical ancestors of the whole family than do the south-west Australian endemics, which seem to have changed quite markedly since their isolation from the other family members (see page 98). The kangaroo paws are the most unusual family members, and seem to have evolved the most.

Haemodoraceae: an old southern family

There are genera of the family Haemodoraceae distributed across South Africa and the Americas (illustrated in colour pages 98-99). South Africa has three small genera, *Barbaretta* (one species) from Natal, and *Dilatris* (five) and *Wachendorfia* (five) from the Cape Region. The New World tropics have three genera, *Xiphidium* (two species) ranging from Bolivia and Brazil to Cuba and Mexico, *Pyrrorhiza* (one) from Amazonian Venezuela, and *Schiekia* (one) from mountainous massifs in Venezuela and Guyana. The genus *Lachnanthes*, with one species, ranges from Nova Scotia to Louisiana in eastern North America, and Cuba. *Lachnanthes*, or red root, was esteemed as a source of an invigorating tonic with narcotic effects by the Seminole Indians of what is now Georgia and Florida. Some medicinal properties, including relief of rheumatism and fever, have been attributed to the species. Ecologically, *Lachnanthes caroliniana* in the south-eastern USA is very similar to *Anigozanthos flavidus* in south-western Australia, being a vigorous coloniser

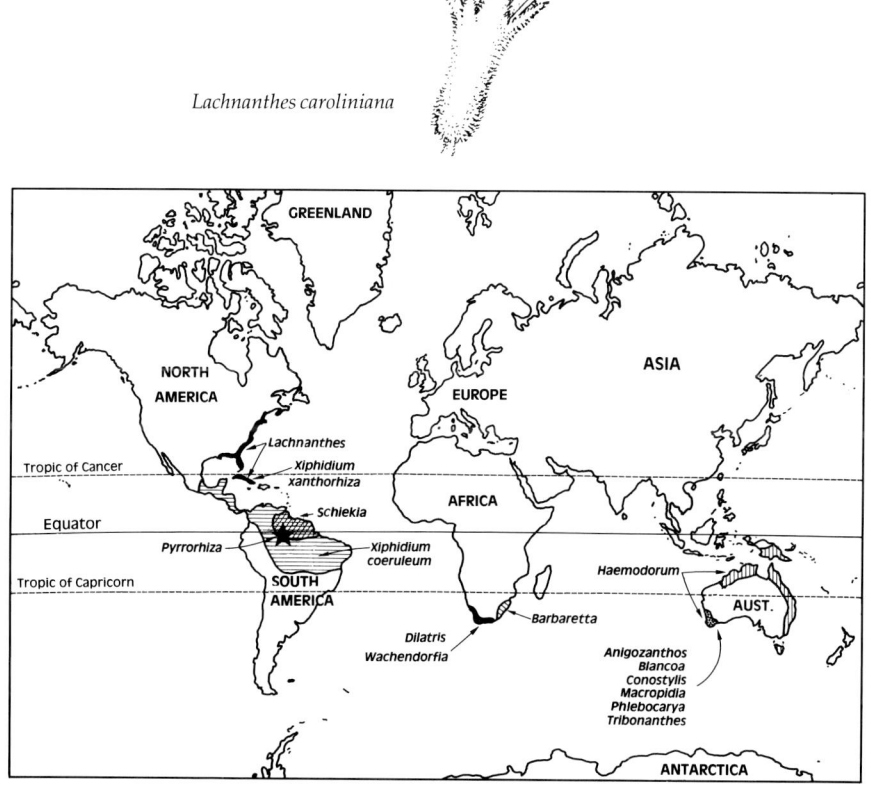

Lachnanthes caroliniana

Further reading

Green, N (ed.) (1979). *Nyungar—The People. Aboriginal Customs in the Southwest of Australia.* (Creative Research, North Perth.)

Macfarlane, T.D., Hopper, S.D., Purdie, R.W., George, A.S. and Patrick, S.J. (1987). Haemodoraceae. *Flora of Australia* **45**, 55–57.

Simpson, M.G. (1983). Pollen ultrastructure of the Haemodoraceae and its taxonomic significance. *Grana* **22**, 79–103.

Simpson, M.G. (1990). Phylogeny and classification of the Haemodoraceae. *Annals of the Missouri Botanical Garden* **77**, 722–784.

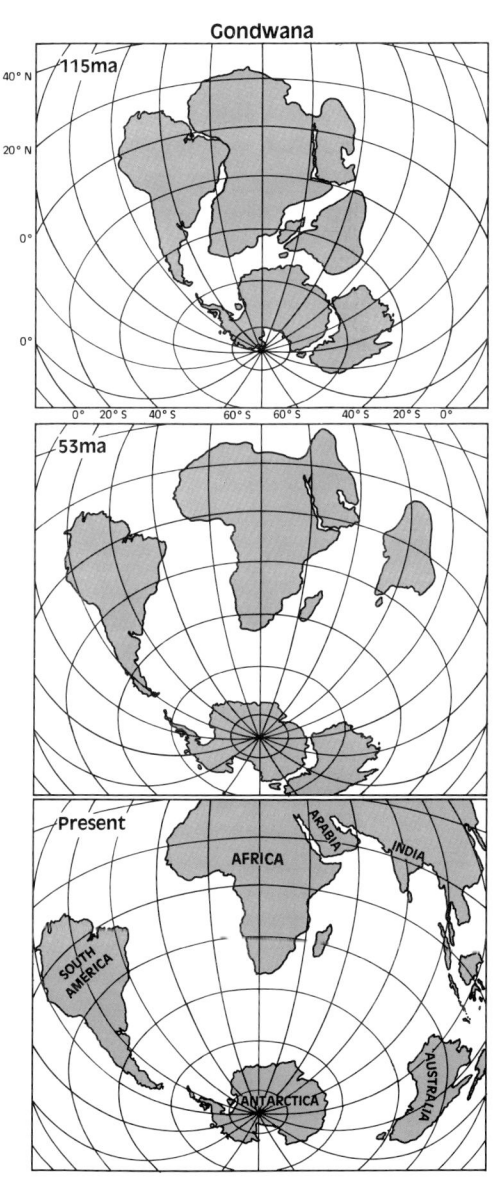

Gondwana and the birth of the southern continents

The broad distributions of many southern hemisphere plant and animal groups reflect the fact that the lands that we know today as Australasia, Africa, Madagascar, India, Antarctica and South America were once part of the great super-continent known as Gondwana. This explains why the genera that make up a family such as the Haemodoraceae are spread across the globe from Australasia to the Americas. The movement into North America of southern hemisphere groups such as *Lachnanthes* (Haemodoraceae) and the Opossum (marsupials) presumably occurred after the break up of Gondwana, when South America joined up with North America just 3-5 million years ago. The three maps show Gondwana 115 million years ago (top), and its continental fragments 53 million years ago and today.

Perianths of the kangaroo paws opened out to show the stamens

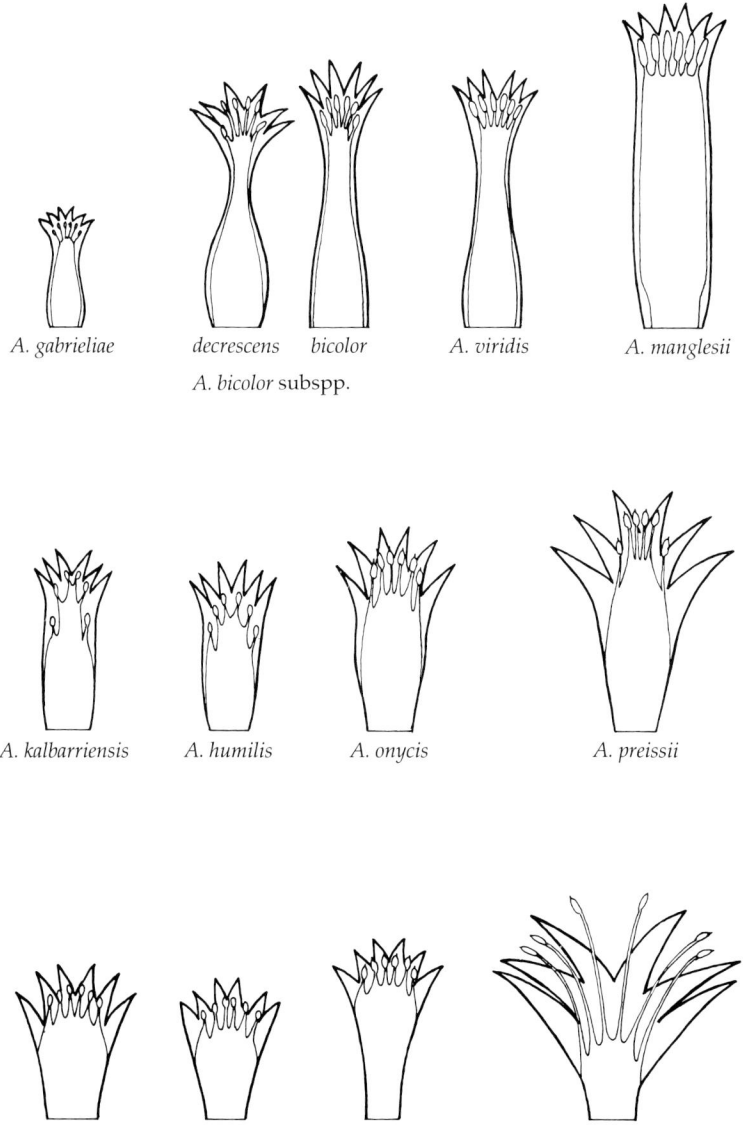

The unique kangaroo paws

There are many features that make the kangaroo paws unique and instantly recognisable. Most are adaptations to the seasonally harsh environment of Western Australia's south-west, such as their tough underground stems, hardy seeds and bright, nectar-laden flowers.

A. manglesii

From little seeds . . .

The seeds of the kangaroo paws are irregular in shape, wingless and hard-coated, ideally suited to persist in the soil close to the parent plant for many years. In *Anigozanthos* species, they range from just 0.5 mm long to 2 mm long, and may be black, grey, grey–brown or red–brown. The number in each fruit ranges from three or four to more than 140.

The seeds of the black kangaroo paw *Macropidia fuliginosa* are very distinctive, being much larger than those of *Anigozanthos* species (up to 5 mm long), with a prominent ridge on the inner surface. Each *Macropidia* fruit contains a maximum of three seeds.

A. viridis

When ripe, each *Macropidia* seed falls away from the fruit with part of the ovary wall and its black hairs attached. In contrast, seeds of most *Anigozanthos* species fall from splits along the top of the ovary wall when shaken by the wind (see page 97). However, *A. rufus* and *A. pulcherrimus* retain their seeds in the fruit, which falls away with the old perianth attached and blows about on the ground. The seeds are released when the perianth wears.

A. flavidus

The seeds of many Australian plants, such as wattles and peas, have fleshy attachments that are attractive to ants. Such seeds are collected by ants and carried into their underground nests, where they are discarded once their attachments have been consumed. This aids the dispersal and colonisation of the plant. The kangaroo paws have not evolved such a mechanism, but there is some evidence that their seeds may be consumed by insect predators.

Macropidia

Kangaroo paw seeds can persist in the soil for many years, and the factors that stimulate them to germinate are poorly understood. The seeds of most species respond to fire, and germination is usually most pronounced following the first autumn rains after a bushfire. A single slender seedling leaf is produced, and often carries the seed coat upwards about a centimetre above the soil on its recurved tip. Next come the first true leaves, which are erect and clustered into a slender, flattened fan. As these grow and increase in number they start to provide the plant with energy, allowing the small underground stem, or rhizome, to swell and begin producing additional fans of leaves.

Mature leaves of the kangaroo paws vary in size, shape and colour sufficiently so as to enable almost all species to be recognised by their leaves alone. For

Seeds of *Macropidia* and *Anigozanthos* species

Left: The shape and size of the perianth, and the placement of stamens inside it, are useful characteristics for identifying the species of kangaroo paws and catspaws, and their hybrids

A. preissii

A. onycis

A. humilis

A. bicolor

Seeds of Anigozanthos species

example, *A. flavidus* has large, flat, evergreen leaves, up to 100 cm long and 2 cm wide. Those of *A. viridis* are almost round in cross-section, grey–green in colour, and are only 10 cm long by 2 mm wide in subspecies *terraspectans*. The common catspaw *A. humilis* has distinctively curved but flat leaves.

All kangaroo paw species have tough, irregular, underground stems called rhizomes, buried 2–10 cm below the soil surface. These are a special adaptation to the hot, dry summers of the south-west, and they also allow the plants to survive summer bushfires. In most species, the leaves and scapes die back after the flowering season so that only the underground rhizome remains over the summer. With the onset of autumn rains, new leaves sprout from the rhizome. In some of the larger species such as *A. flavidus*, *A. pulcherrimus* and *Macropidia fuliginosa*, leaves persist throughout the year and the rhizomes become well established, growing to 5 cm in diameter. Such plants can persist in the same spot for many years. Leaf clusters of individual *A. flavidus* plants may exceed two metres in diameter and live for 30 years or more.

The elusive catspaws

In species such as the catspaws *A. humilis*, *A. kalbarriensis*, *A. preissii* and *A. onycis*, plants are short-lived, surviving no more than one or two growing seasons. They germinate, grow and flower over the autumn, winter and spring following a summer fire. They may persist and flower the next season as well, but few plants do, and they are usually smaller and less vigorous than in their first year. Consequently, such species produce few fans of leaves, and individuals rarely exceed 20 cm in diameter.

Their inability to survive more than one or two years makes some of these short-lived species particularly hard to find in the wild. For example, the branched catspaw *A. onycis* was not seen in the Fitzgerald River National Park in unburnt vegetation for more than 30 years, until a devastating fire late in 1989 stimulated prolific germination of dormant seeds. The species had completely disappeared again by 1991.

Flowering

The flower head in kangaroo paws is termed an inflorescence. An erect flowering stem or scape emerges from the centre of the leaf fan and produces either a widely branched cluster of inflorescences (for example, *A. flavidus*, *Macropidia*), a pair of inflorescences on a short terminal branch (*A. preissii*), or a single, terminal inflorescence (for example, *A. humilis*, *A. viridis*).

These flowering stems range from less than 15 cm tall to more than 3 m, depending on the species. They are usually covered in colourful hairs. In the wild, plants produce 1–5 stems, although *A. flavidus* produces about 10 per plant. In cultivation these numbers may increase tenfold under good conditions.

Parts of the kangaroo paw plant

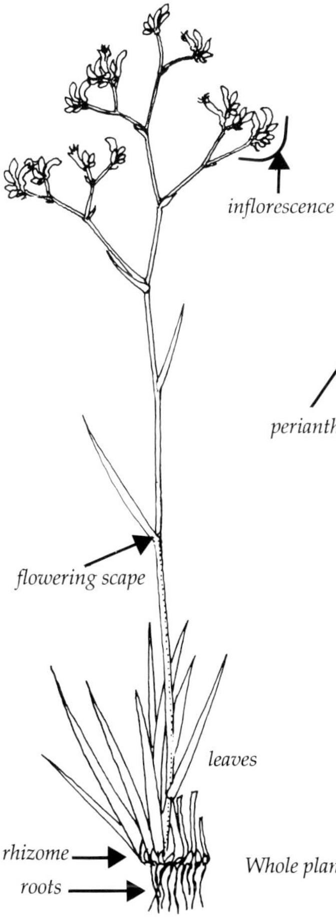

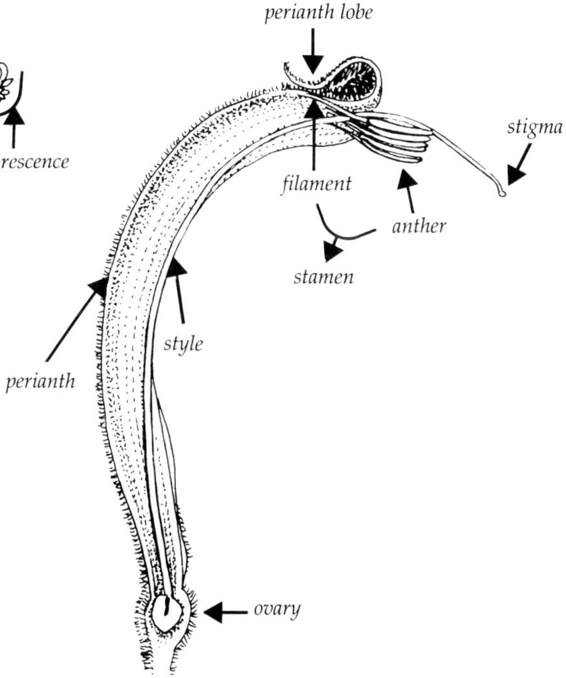

Flower of A. manglesii *shown in cross-section*

Whole plant of A. pulcherrimus

The kangaroo paw plant comprises roots, rhizome (underground stem), leaves, flowering scape and inflorescences. Each inflorescence is composed of several buds and flowers. Each flower has a basal ovary, containing three compartments (locules), each with a central placenta covered in ovules. Out of the ovary arises a slender, elongated structure called the style, at the top of which is a small viscous knob called the stigma. Above the ovary is the main body of the flower, called the perianth, which is covered in brightly coloured, branched hairs. It is tubular for part or most of its length, acting as a container for the nectar. Its other main function is to hold the pollen-bearing anthers in an appropriate position to transfer pollen onto pollinators, and to hold the style so that pollinators place pollen on the stigma while they feed on nectar. Each anther is carried on a short stalk called the filament. The anthers and filaments together are known as the stamens.

The inflorescence is many-flowered and all the buds and fresh flowers face the same direction. The flower heads of *A. preissii* are fairly sparse, carrying only 1–3 flowers per inflorescence. But most species produce denser clusters of flowers, averaging 5–15 per inflorescence. Occasionally, the inflorescences of species such as *A. manglesii* may be laden with as many as 20 flowers.

Usually, only one or two flowers on each inflorescence are open and functional at any given time. The flowers open from the bottom of the inflorescence upwards, and the majority of new flowers open at night. Fresh flowers are thrust forward, usually towards the stem on which pollinators perch. They last up to six days, then lose their colour and rotate sideways so that a pollinator will have access to the next fresh flower above.

In the wild most species produce between 10 and 100 flowers per plant in a season. *A. preissii* is exceptionally thrifty, producing about five flowers or fewer. *A. flavidus* is at the other extreme, averaging around 350 flowers per plant. In cultivation, plants of *A. flavidus* regularly produce more than 2 000 flowers in a season, and some of its hybrids have been recorded as having up to 7 600 flowers.

Flowering is most pronounced in all species following fire. It often tapers off dramatically in subsequent years. The flowering of some species peaks in late winter or early spring (*A. humilis, A. kalbarriensis, A. manglesii, A. viridis, A. bicolor, A. gabrieliae, A. onycis, Macropidia fuliginosa*). The Albany catspaw *A. preissii* peaks in mid or late spring. The remainder peak in late spring or early summer (*A. flavidus, A. rufus, A. pulcherrimus*).

Flower power

When you need to attract a mate, it does not pay to be modest. Many of the most dazzling sights in nature, such as the flamboyant peacock's tail, are designed to give their owners the edge in the mating game. The kangaroo paws are no exception to this rule.

A New Holland honeyeater taking nectar and picking up pollen from A. viridis

The brightly coloured flowers catch the eye of passing pollinators, who are attracted by the promise of a nectar feast. Nectar production in some species is among the highest known for plants. *Macropidia*, for example, may produce an average of 170 μL per flower each day. Some flowers of *A. manglesii* produce 250 μL of nectar per day. Other species are less productive, for example, *A. humilis* averages only 10–20 μL of nectar. The nectar typically contains 5–20% sugar, offering pollinators a rich energy source.

But there is no such thing as a free lunch, and in pushing down the tubular perianth to feed on the nectar, the pollinators will inevitably brush against the anthers, and pick up some pollen. Pollen production is copious, especially in the large anthers of *A. manglesii*, which may be up to 12 mm long. The pollen grains, which are sausage-shaped, remain functional for only a day after being released from the anthers.

With any luck, the hungry pollinator will move on to feed on another plant of the same species, and will unknowingly transfer the pollen from its head and nape onto the stigma of the next flower. The stigma is receptive only for the first few days after the flower opens, which coincides with the peak of nectar production. After that its surface dries up, and it is no longer functional. Provided the stigma is receptive, the pollen grains will germinate (see page 50) and their pollen tubes will grow down the style into the ovary, where they will fertilise the ovules. The fertilised ovules develop into seeds.

Further reading

Dixon, I.R. (1983). The propagation of *Macropidia fuliginosa* from seed. In *The Production and Marketing of Australian Wildflowers for Export*, pp. 56–69. (University Extension, The University of Western Australia, Perth.)

Grieve, B.J. and Marchant, N. (1963). The kangaroo paws of WA. *Australian Plants* **2**, 107–115.

Hopper, S.D. (1978). *Speciation in the Kangaroo Paws of South-western Australia* (Anigozanthos *and* Macropidia: *Haemodoraceae).* PhD thesis (The University of Western Australia, Perth).

Hopper, S.D. (1987). *Blancoa, Anigozanthos, Macropidia. Flora of Australia* **45**, 110–128.

Hopper, S.D. and Campbell, N.A. (1977). A multivariate morphometric study of species relationships in kangaroo paws (*Anigozanthos* Labill. and *Macropidia* Drumm. ex Harv.: Haemodoraceae). *Australian Journal of Botany* **25**, 523–544.

Pate, J.S. and Hopper, S.D. (1993). Rare and common plants in ecosystems, with special reference to the south-west Australian flora. In D. Schultze and H. Mooney (eds), *Biodiversity and Ecosystem Function*. (Springer Verlag.) In press.

Sukhvibul, N. (1991). *Study on Improvement of Red and Green Kangaroo Paw* (Anigozanthos manglesii *D.Don).* MSc thesis (The University of Western Australia, Perth).

Where to find kangaroo paws

Like all plants, the kangaroo paws have certain soil and climate preferences, but if you are in the south-west of Western Australia anywhere between the coast and the wheatbelt in late winter to early summer, you should be able to find some if you look in the right places.

The region termed the south-west of Western Australia (WA) takes in an area from Shark Bay north of Perth to Israelite Bay east of Esperance. The kangaroo paws and catspaws range widely throughout this region, and one (*A. rufus*) is even found further east, on isolated sand patches towards the head of the Great Australian Bight. The species are limited mainly to areas between the coast and the wheatbelt, where annual rainfall is more than about 500 mm. They do not generally penetrate as far inland as the central and eastern wheatbelt and adjacent arid interior.

As the kangaroo paws require direct sunlight, they mainly inhabit the heathland and mallee heath areas of the south-west, known locally as *kwongan* (an Aboriginal word from the Nyungar language). A few species penetrate the high-rainfall open woodland regions, but only the evergreen kangaroo paw is tolerant enough of shade to inhabit the tall karri, jarrah and marri forests.

Distribution

The common catspaw is the species that ranges across the widest area, from Kalbarri National Park as far south as Dunsborough and south-east to Hopetoun, avoiding only the high-rainfall forests. At the other extreme, the Mogumber catspaw has a very narrow distribution, being confined to an area of just a few square kilometres at the foot of the Darling Scarp.

From the Stirling Range to Albany there are hundreds of different varieties of wildflowers. This is one of the areas richest in kangaroo paw species. The impressive peaks of the Stirling Range overlook foothills and plains that support five species of kangaroo paw (*A. humilis, A. rufus, A. gabrieliae, A. onycis* and *A. bicolor*), with *A. manglesii* close by at Kendenup. Southwards, near Albany, *A. preissii, A. flavidus* and *A. bicolor* can be found.

The Lesueur National Park, on the sandplains east of Jurien Bay, has a hugely varied flora. The vegetation is mainly *kwongan*, and *A. humilis, A. pulcherrimus, A. manglesii* and *Macropidia* grow there. A little further south towards Cervantes and Cataby, *A. viridis* may also be found. Further north, Kalbarri National Park is famous for its wildflowers. There are three species of kangaroo paw there: *A. humilis, A. manglesii* and *A. kalbarriensis*. The latter is found only in the heath north and south of the Murchison River, an area which includes the National Park.

Branched catspaws growing in recently burnt jarrah–Kingia *open woodland*

There is an extensive network of national parks and reserves in the Perth Metropolitan Region, which is well endowed with kangaroo paws. *A. humilis, A. manglesii* and *A. viridis* grow on the coastal plain, and *A. bicolor* in the Darling Range. Kings Park covers 400 hectares in the heart of Perth, two-thirds of which is bushland. In the spring there are kangaroo paws everywhere in the Park.

Areas where just one species predominates include the high-rainfall southern giant karri forests. The robust evergreen *A. flavidus* is capable of competing against vigorous understorey species in the rich soils of karri forests after fire. All the other kangaroo paw species are excluded because of their need for full sun and well-drained sandy soils. In the drier western margins of the wheatbelt, *A. humilis* is better able than any other species to grow and flower during the short growing season. It is puzzling that this species has not penetrated the southern coastal sandplains eastwards beyond Hopetoun. Perhaps the occurrence of summer rainfall near the south coast does not favour *A. humilis*. Eastwards from the Israelite Bay area, *A. rufus* is the sole species of kangaroo paw present. It occupies an isolated sand patch on the edge of the Nullarbor Plain at Point Culver.

Habitats

The south-west region incorporates a wide variety of climatic and soil conditions, and the kangaroo paw species thrive in some and struggle in others. They occupy a range of different habitats, but are especially common in sandy soils. They vary in their tolerance of water. Swamp margins and winter-wet flats are the preferred home of *A. viridis, A. flavidus, A. bicolor* and *A. gabrieliae*. All may be found growing partly submersed during winter or spring rains.

Species preferring a little less water, but still found near moist sites, include *A. rufus, A. pulcherrimus, A. manglesii* and *A. kalbarriensis*. Well-drained soils on slopes and hilltops are favoured by *A. preissii, A. humilis, A. onycis* and *Macropidia fuliginosa*. The black kangaroo paw is not restricted to sandy soils, and is notable in its ability to occupy hilltops composed of laterite gravel conglomerate. *A. flavidus* is particularly adaptable, and is able to grow well in clay-loams as well as peaty sands, and may even grow partly immersed in brackish estuarine water along the south coast.

Although they may not compete effectively with established communities of tall shrubs and trees, all species are fire opportunists. They appear in greatest numbers in habitats disturbed by fire, or by other processes that remove the canopy of trees and shrubs, allowing more light to reach the soil. You will often find them growing along bulldozed or burnt road verges. *A. flavidus* is exceptionally tolerant of competition. Indeed, it is the weediest and most robust coloniser among the kangaroo paws, sometimes dominating road verges in the tall forests of the south-west region.

Further reading

Grieve, B.J. and Marchant, N. (1963). The kangaroo paws of W.A. *Australian Plants* **2**, 107–115.

Hopper, S.D. (1978). *Speciation in the Kangaroo Paws of South-western Australia (*Anigozanthos *and* Macropidia: *Haemodoraceae).* PhD thesis (The University of Western Australia, Perth).

Hopper, S.D. (1987). *Blancoa, Anigozanthos, Macropidia. Flora of Australia* **45**, 110–128.

Strategies for coping with fire

The first winter–spring after a bush fire, sprouter species such as *Macropidia* (illustrated) may grow from established rhizomes or germinate from seed. Short-lived seeder species such as *A. onycis* (illustrated) do not resprout from rhizomes. Instead they germinate from seeds, and flower prolifically. In the second year after a fire, sprouter species reach their flowering peak, establishing a larger rhizome and a bank of seeds in the soil. In the years that follow the plants persist, flowering sporadically. In contrast, by the second year after a fire only a few plants of seeder species persist, and from the third year onwards the plants have completely disappeared. Most plants of seeder species only survive for one year after a fire, but they leave a good store of seeds in the soil.

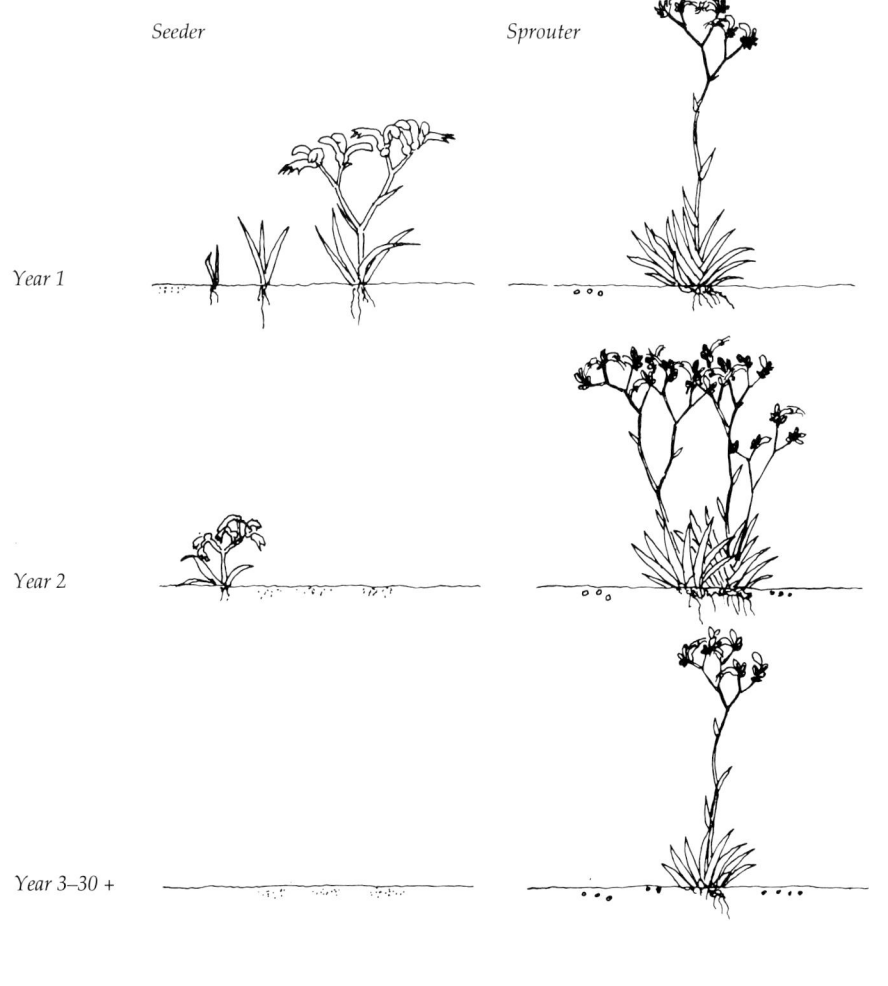

Seeders and sprouters

To the kangaroo paws, fire is a potent force that orchestrates their life cycles. They have two distinct strategies that enable them not only to survive fires, but to take advantage of the temporarily empty landscape that fire leaves behind.

Fire is a pervasive and recurrent feature of the strongly seasonal environment of the south-west of Western Australia. With the onset of each long, dry summer, vegetation becomes fire-prone, and the risk of fire remains high until the autumn rains arrive.

Few plant communities escape the reach of fire, and some experience it at regular intervals, largely at the hands of humans. It is likely that fire has been a significant environmental factor in the south-west since the climatic changes that brought the onset of aridity several million years ago, long before the first human occupation.

The living fire

There are two major strategies for coping with fire that are adopted by plants. These strategies are best described by the terms 'seeders' and 'sprouters'.

When 'seeder' species are killed by canopy fire, they are entirely reliant for regeneration on the hardy seeds that they leave behind in the soil. By contrast, 'sprouter' species are capable of resprouting after fire from underground roots or protected buds in trunks and branches. Sprouters may also regenerate from seeds, so they have two modes of reproduction.

Thus, sprouters are able to regenerate after a fire, even if they have not had time to flower and produce seeds. Seeders are more vulnerable. They have to have time to germinate, grow to maturity and produce seeds in between fires. A short fire interval could eradicate a seeder species.

Although the terms seeder and sprouter are usually applied to woody plants, the different strategies are well illustrated by the kangaroo paws. The short-lived species, including all of the catspaws (with the probable exceptions of the Mogumber catspaw and the giant catspaw), as well as species such as *A. gabrieliae* and some subspecies of *A. bicolor*, are classic seeders. They grow rapidly, and within a year or two of a fire have produced a reserve of seeds sufficient for regeneration, after which they die (see Chapter 3).

In contrast, several of the branched species, including *Macropidia, A. flavidus, A. rufus* and *A. pulcherrimus*, are much longer-lived. They often take two years from fire to reach their full flowering potential, but persist for many years thereafter, developing a well-established rhizome. Typically, these species resprout vigorously from the rhizome after fire (see Chapter 3).

Fire ecology

When a summer fire destroys the bush, the landscape often comes alive with colour the following spring. The seeder species of kangaroo paw often carpet the sun-drenched, charcoal-enriched soil, but their splendour is transient. The next spring only a few stragglers are seen, and from then on virtually none, until the next fire triggers massive germination of seeds.

The sprouter species, too, may form large colourful populations for a year or two after a fire. Then, as the shrubs and trees become re-established, the kangaroo paws must compete for sunlight and only scattered individuals persist, in sites not entirely shaded out by the shrubby regrowth.

Fire as a force for change

In evolutionary terms, the sprouting species of kangaroo paws are probably closer to the form of the ancestral kangaroo paws than are the seeder species. Most other genera of the Haemodoraceae family are sprouters, indicating that this is probably the original mode of regeneration for the family. The seeder lifestyle results in more rapid turnover of generations, and hence faster evolutionary change, than that of the sprouters. This is illustrated by the greater floral variation and racial divergence seen in seeder species of *Anigozanthos* than in sprouters (see Chapter 9).

Because of this explosive evolutionary divergence, distinct subspecies are found in most seeder species, such as *A. humilis* and *A. bicolor*. In contrast, there is no significant geographical variation in sprouters such as *A. flavidus*, *Macropidia* or *A. rufus*.

Interestingly, in *A. humilis* the widespread subspecies *humilis* is a seeder, whereas the other two subspecies are quite rare, localised, and are probably sprouters. This may be a living example of the evolution from sprouter to seeder within the same species.

Much remains to be learnt about the fire ecology of the kangaroo paws and catspaws, but a knowledge of this significant environmental force is undoubtedly central to understanding the natural history of these plants.

Further reading

Baird, A. M. (1977). Regeneration after fire in Kings Park, Perth, Western Australia. *Journal of the Royal Society of Western Australia* **60**, 1–22.

Baird, A. M. (1984). Observations on regeneration after fire in the Yule Brook Reserve near Perth, Western Australia. *Journal of the Royal Society of Western Australia* **66**, 147–162.

Bell, D.T., Hopkins, A.J.M. and Pate, J.S. (1984). Fire in the kwongan. In J.S. Pate and J.S. Beard (eds), *Kwongan — Plant Life of the Sandplain*, pp. 178–204. (University of Western Australia Press, Perth.)

Pate, J.S. and Hopper, S.D. (1993). Rare and common plants in ecosystems, with special reference to the south-west Australian flora. In D. Schultze and H. Mooney (eds), *Biodiversity and Ecosystem Function*. (Springer Verlag.) In press.

Runciman, H.V. (1989). *The Conservation Biology of Two Species of Kangaroo Paw*. MAppSc thesis (Curtin University of Technology, Perth).

Kangaroo paws and pollinators

Kangaroo paws and catspaws are pollinated by birds and marsupials. The shorter species are pollinated mainly by birds standing on the ground, whereas the taller species require their pollinators to perch on the stems. Because of the success with which kangaroo paws attract pollinators, they are extremely efficient at reproduction. Populations of *A. manglesii, A. humilis, A. bicolor, A. viridis* and *Macropidia* have been found to have 50–90% of their flowers successfully pollinated and setting seed. In *A. flavidus*, with its greater capacity to set seed on self-pollination, 97% of flowers are successfully pollinated.

Pollination

There is a fascinating interplay between the kangaroo paws and their unwitting pollinators, in which the plants are by no means simply the passive partners. They exhibit a range of striking adaptations that increase the chance of successful pollination.

The south-west of Western Australia has a remarkably large number of plants adapted for pollination by birds and mammals. It has been estimated that 15% of south-western wildflowers are pollinated by birds and mammals, compared with only 7% of wildflowers in tropical WA, and 6% of the desert flora. This contrasts dramatically with Europe, which has no flowers that are pollinated by birds or mammals (most are pollinated by insects or by the wind). Mainland USA has a small number of plant species that are pollinated by hummingbirds. Tropical countries tend to have more bird-pollinated species, and have some species that are pollinated by bats, monkeys and other mammals, but none can match the diversity of bird-pollinated plants seen in the south-west of Western Australia.

The kangaroo paws and catspaws are supremely well adapted to pollination by birds and mammals. Their striking colours and large robust flowers with copious nectar attract vertebrates seeking food, enabling the movement of pollen from plant to plant. Vertebrate pollinators are fussy in their feeding habits, and invariably explore fresh, brightly coloured, open flowers, ignoring the dull closed ones below on the inflorescence. This is presumably because nectar is only produced over the first few days, when flowers are freshly open. Not surprisingly, the timing of this tempting feast coincides with the release of pollen from splits in the anthers, and the time when the stigma is receptive and able to facilitate the germination of pollen grains.

Most kangaroo paws and catspaws need pollinators that move frequently from plant to plant, because self-pollination of flowers from the same plant yields very poor seed set in all species except *A. flavidus*. Even in the latter species, cross-pollination of separate plants produces many more seeds than does self-pollination. Hence, cross-pollination is almost obligatory in most species and, as we shall discuss later, certain species have developed striking adaptations that reduce the risk of self-pollination.

Marsupials

Nectar-feeding marsupials are a special group of animals found in the south-west of WA. Indeed, the mouse-sized honey possum is found nowhere else. This is the only mammal in the world that lives exclusively on a diet of nectar and pollen. The less common western pygmy possum also feeds at flowers, but will eat many other food items as well.

There has been no detailed study on the importance of mammals as pollinators of the kangaroo paws. Captive honey possums will readily feed on flowers of *A. rufus* (see photo page 143), and honey possums caught in the wild near Jurien were found to have pollen from *A. pulcherrimus* on their fur. A recent study also showed that nectar volumes in *A. pulcherrimus* and *Macropidia* declined overnight, suggesting that nocturnal honey possums were active at flowers before nectar-feeding birds began feeding at dawn. Careful field and laboratory studies are needed to gain a sound understanding of this intriguing relationship.

Honeyeaters

Honeyeaters are the main group of Australian nectar-feeding birds, and there are some 21 species in the south-west. In a recent survey of the wildlife of Perth, about 80% of all individual birds counted were honeyeaters. Their melodious calls and engaging, but aggressive, chasing are familiar features of our landscape.

We have a much better understanding of the importance of birds in the pollination of kangaroo paws and catspaws than we do of mammals. Honeyeaters have been recorded feeding on flowers of most species, and they appear to be highly efficient as pollinators. But if nectar is readily available from different species in the same habitat, honeyeaters can be quite indiscriminate in their feeding behaviour. Such indiscriminate feeding is wasteful of a plant's pollen, and may clog stigmas with foreign pollen, thereby reducing seed production.

Avoiding self-pollination

The kangaroo paws and catspaws achieve more selective pollination, and thereby increase their reproductive output, through a number of striking adaptations. The fact that kangaroo paws can grow and flower after fire more rapidly than most other bird-pollinated plants, means that they enjoy a near monopoly of the foraging time of honeyeaters at such times. Species that occur in low heathland or very open mallee heath, and that flower best after fire, are often pollinated by a single species of honeyeater specialised for that habitat: the tawny-crowned honeyeater. This small acrobatic bird has been observed feeding on dense stands of *A. onycis* in Fitzgerald River National Park, on stands of *A. gabrieliae* in the Stirling Range, and on *A. viridis* subsp. *terraspectans* near Cataby. In each case, the kangaroo paws were the only bird-pollinated plants in flower in the recently burnt habitat, and the tawny-crowned honeyeaters were the only active pollinator.

Another kangaroo paw species that enjoys a monopoly of the pollinator in a specific habitat is *A. preissii* in Albany blackbutt (*Eucalyptus staeri*) low woodland. The scattered solitary pollinators of *A. preissii* are western spinebills. These spectacularly coloured birds are among the smallest honeyeaters, and

Feeding behaviour of tawny-crowned honeyeaters

Tawny-crowned honeyeaters are often the only species found in low heathland or open mallee heath. Therefore, after fire when kangaroo paws such as *A. onycis* (illustrated) appear, tawny-crowned honeyeaters are the only pollinator. They usually perch on dead sticks, then drop to the ground to feed. They feed standing on the ground, or perching a few centimetres above the ground on the flowering stems, feeding on 1–3 flowers per plant. They might move up to 8 m, hopping on the ground from plant to plant, before ascending a perch, flying 20–40 m, and dropping down to feed on the kangaroo paws again. Such behaviour guarantees a high level of cross-pollination between plants, which ensures a greater yield of seed.

are able to live on very small amounts of nectar (see pages 41 and 143). The flowers produced by *A. preissii* offer only limited nectar, and honeyeaters larger than western spinebills are presumably unable to obtain enough food from them, and migrate to richer and more concentrated nectar sources.

When it is at its densest immediately after fire, *A. preissii* can produce six plants and eight open flowers per square metre, but averages less than one plant with one open flower per square metre in a normal post-fire population. It is usually the earliest bird-pollinated plant to flower after a fire. The cross-pollination rate between plants must be very high in *A. preissii*, possibly the highest in the genus, because the species produces only one open flower per plant on average. On the few occasions on which pollination has been observed, the western spinebills fed on a few flowers consecutively, moving several metres between plants while doing so.

Several species are adapted to producing a small number of open flowers, which is clearly advantageous in terms of reducing the chance of self-pollination. For example, *Macropidia*, the black kangaroo paw, produces an average of one flower or less per square metre. *A. pulcherrimus* produces higher averages, between 10 and 100 per square metre, depending upon the density of the plants.

In contrast with the restrained flowering of *A. preissii* and *Macropidia*, *A. flavidus* produces an abundance of flowers. Its many-branched flowering stems can carry more than 300 open flowers on a single plant, although they normally carry about 65. New Holland honeyeaters are a common pollinator, and in karri–marri forest near Witchcliffe, they have been seen feeding on up to 50 flowers on the same plant before moving a few metres to the next one. Clearly, a lot more self-pollination occurs in this situation, but as *A. flavidus* is more tolerant of this than most other species, it is still able to set reasonable numbers of seed.

Shifting pollinators

A particular kangaroo paw or catspaw species may be pollinated by different species of honeyeaters at different locations, habitats or times. New Holland honeyeaters are the most common pollinators of *A. flavidus*, but other honeyeaters appear sporadically. Grant Wardell-Johnson, a Department of Conservation and Land Management (CALM) scientist, observed that western spinebills and brown honeyeaters did not occur in dense karri forest in the Hilltops area of Walpole-Nornalup National Park until after a fire in 1987. Following this fire, *A. flavidus* carpeted the understorey, and both species of bird appeared from adjacent coastal communities to feed on this unexpected banquet of nectar. Similarly, western spinebills were the major pollinators of *A. flavidus* after a fire near One Tree Bridge in the Donnelly River area.

It is often the case that more than one species of honeyeater is involved in the pollination of a kangaroo paw species at a particular site. In studies near

Jurien, Elisabeth Brown (a Masters student from Curtin University of Technology) found that three species were active on *A. pulcherrimus*: western spinebills, brown honeyeaters and tawny-crowned honeyeaters. Only four or five open flowers per stem were available to the birds, and they tended to visit most of them before moving to another stem. About four stems were visited on any given feeding bout, and as there were usually only one or two stems per plant, *A. pulcherrimus* received a reasonable amount of cross-pollination through the feeding movements of these birds. White-cheeked honeyeaters have also been seen feeding on this species.

In the case of *Macropidia*, Elisabeth Brown observed three species of pollinators near Jurien: tawny-crowned honeyeaters, singing honeyeaters and brown

More flowers attract more pollinators

Interestingly, denser stands of kangaroo paws seem to attract more attention from honeyeaters. Elisabeth Brown found that honeyeaters visited the flowers of *A. pulcherrimus* and *Macropidia* more often, and moved between plants more frequently in high-density populations than in those of low density. However, no differences in the number of fruit set were found between the high and low density populations of either species. Therefore, honeyeater visits were still sufficient to ensure pollination of most flowers in the low-density populations. (Visits from honey possums may have been helping as well.)

honeyeaters. The black kangaroo paws had two or three open flowers per stem and only one or two stems per plant. Its pollinators tended to visit all the open flowers on a plant, but travelled further from plant to plant than the birds pollinating *A. pulcherrimus*, as the *Macropidia* population was less dense. It seems likely that *Macropidia* is more extensively cross-pollinated than is *A. pulcherrimus*, because it grows less densely, and has fewer open flowers per stem than *A. pulcherrimus*. White-cheeked honeyeaters have also been seen feeding on *Macropidia*.

To get an idea of whether the species of pollinators visiting a site change over time, a population of *A. manglesii, A. humilis* and some rare hybrids was studied during 10 of the years between 1976 and 1992. The plants were growing in the cemetery grounds at Gingin, north of Perth. In 1976, several red wattlebirds dominated the nectar supply of both kangaroo paw species, chasing away the occasional brown honeyeater and yellow-throated miner that attempted to feed. However, during the nine other recorded years, no one species of honeyeater was observed to have such complete dominance. A few brown honeyeaters were seen on every occasion that the cemetery population was inspected, but they only fed on *A. manglesii*. Occasional New Holland honeyeaters were seen in the flowering seasons of 1978, 1980 and 1986. These, too, were only seen feeding on *A. manglesii*. Red wattlebirds were observed during five of the 10 recorded years. They fed mainly on *A. manglesii*, but also on *A. humilis* and, very occasionally, on the hybrids. A little wattlebird was seen once in 1986 and again in 1988. Feeding was not observed. A western spinebill appeared in 1982 and 1983, but has not been seen since. A few silvereyes were seen on only one occasion throughout the study. They fed on *A. manglesii*.

These observations illustrate the dynamic changes in pollinators from year to year in some kangaroo paw populations. Honeyeaters can move long distances in search of nectar, and clearly do so in the agricultural landscape that surrounds Gingin cemetery. Only the smallest honeyeaters, such as brown honeyeaters and western spinebills, are likely to remain in an area when nectar supplies are low. Larger species such as the wattlebirds simply have to move on to satisfy their greater need for food and energy. Hence, it is perhaps not surprising that brown honeyeaters were always seen at Gingin cemetery, whereas all other species came and went.

The discerning honeyeater

In many places, such as at Gingin, two, three, or even four species of kangaroo paw may grow together in mixed stands, or adjacent to each other. How do honeyeaters behave in these situations? Do they stick faithfully to the nectar of one species, or flit indiscriminately back and forth between different species? Studies by the author and Dr Allan Burbidge, a CALM scientist, suggest that it depends upon differences in the heights and flowering seasons of the kangaroo paw species.

At Kendenup near the Stirling Range, honeyeaters were observed feeding at a site where *A. humilis* subsp. *humilis* was growing on gentle sandy rises, *A.bicolor* subsp. *decrescens* on waterlogged flats, and mixed stands of both species and equivalent numbers of hybrids were growing on the intervening slopes. The two species and their hybrids were of similar height (stems averaging 20 cm tall), were all in full flower at the time, and offered similar numbers of open flowers and nectar to the birds. Under these circumstances the pollinators (red wattlebirds and singing honeyeaters) showed no preference for one or other species of kangaroo paw. They just fed indiscriminately on whatever plants were encountered during a feeding session.

To the north-west near Hillman, brown honeyeaters and silvereyes were observed feeding on a mixed population of three species: *A. manglesii* (in full flower), *A. bicolor* (just past full flower) and *A. humilis* (which had almost finished flowering, and therefore received little attention). Hybrids of *A. bicolor* and *A. manglesii* were common (16% of the population). Although *A. manglesii*, *A. bicolor* and their hybrids produced similar volumes of nectar, the two species differed significantly in the height of their flowering stems. *A. manglesii* was largest, averaging 45 cm tall, whereas *A. bicolor* averaged 20 cm, and the hybrids averaged 30 cm. The honeyeaters fed almost exclusively on the tall stems of *A. manglesii*. They dropped down occasionally onto the slightly smaller hybrids, but they were not observed on the small stems of *A. bicolor*. Both brown honeyeaters and silvereyes are small furtive species (see page 41), often chased by larger honeyeaters, and rarely seen feeding far from the cover of dense shrubs or tall trees. Perhaps feeding close to the ground, as on an *A. bicolor* stem, would make them vulnerable to harassment or predation. In any event, when they grow together in mixed stands, the difference in the heights of the flowers of *A. manglesii* and *A. bicolor* clearly has a strong influence on pollination by certain honeyeaters.

This phenomenon was even more evident at the Gingin Shire cemetery in 1976, when red wattlebirds were observed feeding on *A. humilis*, *A. manglesii* and their rare hybrids (0.5% of the population). *A. humilis* reached its flowering peak a month earlier (in August) than *A. manglesii* (September), and had much shorter flowering stems. The red wattlebirds were very discriminating in this population. When *A. humilis* was in full flower, 97% of their movements involved standing on the ground and hopping between plants of this species, often ignoring the scattered taller stems of early flowering *A. manglesii*. A month later, when *A. manglesii* came into full flower, the birds shifted their attention, so that 97% of their movements involved hopping from stem to stem on different *A. manglesii* plants, often over flowers of *A. humilis* below.

Thus, the feeding behaviour of honeyeaters has been observed in a variety of mixed populations at Kendenup, Hillman and Gingin. Where the kangaroo paw species were identical in the height of their flowering stems and in their flowering seasons, the honeyeaters did not discriminate between them. But where species showed substantial differences in these features, there was a corresponding increase in the level of discriminatory or species-specific pollination by the honeyeaters, and a decrease in the relative numbers of hybrids. Under such circumstances, it is clear that a simple shift in the height of flowering stems within a species, for example, could have a profound effect on the behaviour of pollinators, and lead to two breeding groups of plants. It seems probable that new subspecies and species of the kangaroo paws have originated in this way (see Chapter 9).

Study of their pollinators has thus provided insights into why some kangaroo paws are tall and others short, why they flower at different times, and why they might grow only in certain habitats. The flowers that inspire so much human admiration assume even greater meaning when viewed in the context of their ecological and evolutionary functions. The next time you see a kangaroo paw, try examining it from a honeyeater's perspective.

Further reading

Brown, E. (1988). *Pollination and Seed Production in Two Species of Kangaroo Paws,* Anigozanthos pulcherrimus *and* Macropidia fuliginosa. MAppSc thesis (Curtin University of Technology, Perth).

Hopper, S.D. and Burbidge, A.H. (1978). Assortative pollination by red wattlebirds in a hybrid population of *Anigozanthos* Labill. (Haemodoraceae). *Australian Journal of Botany* **26**, 335–350.

Hopper, S.D. and Burbidge, A.H. (1986). Speciation of bird-pollinated plants in south-western Australia. In H.A. Ford and D.C. Paton (eds), *The Dynamic Partnership: Birds and Plants in Southern Australia*, pp. 20–31. (Government Printer, Adelaide.)

Keighery, G.J. (1982). Bird pollinated plants in Western Australia and their breeding systems. In J.A. Armstrong, J.M. Powell and A.J. Richards (eds), *Pollination and Evolution*, pp. 77–89. (Royal Botanic Gardens, Sydney.)

Birds that feed on kangaroo paw nectar

A nectar thief

Parrots sometimes harvest nectar from kangaroo paws, destroying the flowers in the process. Here, a red-capped parrot stands among ravaged flowers of *A. humilis*.

Pollen and nectar poachers

The feast of nectar laid on to tempt pollinators also attracts a range of other animals to kangaroo paw flowers. Most are nectar or pollen thieves and do not assist in pollination.

Living natural ecosystems are composed of animals, plants and micro-organisms that have complex webs of relationships. Not all such relationships are mutually beneficial. The kangaroo paws are surrounded by animals that regard their flowers simply as food, and consume them without achieving pollination. Fortunately, the ability of the kangaroo paws to resprout, and to produce an abundance of seeds, enables the plants to tolerate a certain amount of such unwanted attention.

Peripatetic parrots

At Gingin cemetery in the 1980s, a few red-capped parrots and Port Lincoln parrots became resident, and were seen frequently among the kangaroo paws and catspaws. In September 1980, a couple of red-capped parrots were observed perched on the stems of *A. manglesii*, biting off flowers, chewing the base of the perianth to squeeze out nectar, and then dropping the flowers on the ground. In 1986, red-capped parrots and Port Lincoln parrots were seen standing on the ground and destroying flowers of *A. humilis* to obtain nectar. It was estimated that 90% of all flowers produced by the catspaws that season lay on the ground unpollinated as a result. However, this was exceptional. Over many years of observation throughout the south-west, high levels of parrot predation have rarely been seen, even though both red-capped parrots and Port Lincolns are common and widespread in wooded areas. Port Lincoln parrots have been reported as a pest in plantations of *Macropidia* near Moore River, preferring this species to *A. manglesii*, which they rarely touch.

Bugs and caterpillars

Insects are more frequently observed at kangaroo paw and catspaw flowers than parrots. Tiny thrips are almost universal, but they are so small as to have an inconsequential effect on nectar volumes or pollination. Ants may be seen occasionally, supping nectar, but would also be too small for pollination.

Hairy caterpillars are sometimes found eating the young buds of an inflorescence, but the ancestors of the kangaroo paws evolved potent chemical defences against such herbivory millions of years ago. The tissues of all kangaroo paw species are packed with minute clusters of needle-like calcium oxalate crystals (see page 50). These clusters are called raphides, and they are toxic to most animals. If the caterpillars survive such meals, they probably live to regret it.

Caterpillar consuming floral buds

Night-time thieves

Studies in Perth's Kings Park and Botanic Garden by zoologists Darryl Gwynne, Leigh Simmons and Wynne Bailey from the University of Western Australia, have revealed that two species of long-horned grasshoppers (flightless katydids) are responsible for harvesting the pollen of *A. manglesii*, and destroying many flowers. These slender, stick-like, nocturnal insects hatch in winter. The adults mature in spring, and feed at night entirely on pollen and nectar of species such as stinkbush (*Jacksonia sternbergiana*), milkmaids (*Burchardia umbellata*), balgas or grass trees (*Xanthorrhoea preissii*) and the red and green kangaroo paw *A. manglesii*.

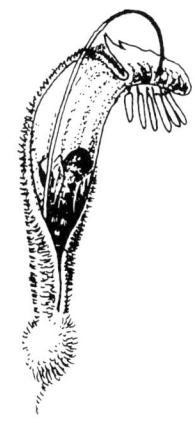

The large anthers and abundance of pollen in *A. manglesii* make it a favoured food of the katydids. The larger of the two katydid species (*Phasmodes ranatriformis*) was described by Darryl as eating in the following way: "This insect straddles the kangaroo paw flowers and 'castrates' them by eating each of the six anthers from top to bottom like a series of popsicles!" The more common smaller species (an unnamed genus and species) is less damaging in its feeding habits, but nevertheless removes a substantial amount of the pollen produced by *A. manglesii* and would rarely pollinate the flowers by its activity.

The two katydid species must have evolved digestive mechanisms that can cope with the harmful effects of the calcium oxalate crystals that they ingest with the pollen and anther tissue. As yet, this aspect of their biology has not been investigated.

The kangaroo paws are used as a mating ground by the katydids. The males have a call that is inaudible to human ears, unlike the raucous clicking and buzzing produced in the summer by their relatives. But the females find the ultrasonic calls attractive, and take time out from feeding on the *A. manglesii* pollen to mate.

The insects display unusual role reversals in sexual behaviour, which are associated with the abundance of pollen as food. The males provide females with additional food as an inducement to mating, in the form of a large protein mass attached to the sperm bundle (see page 143). When normal food such as the kangaroo paw pollen is scarce, males offering the seductive protein mass are the choosy sex, and females compete for males. When food is plentiful the roles reverse; females become choosy and males compete for them. This interesting variation in sexual behaviour has enabled the zoologists to explore the validity of many ideas concerning the evolution of sex.

The kangaroo paw flowers are thus unwilling hosts during important parts of the life cycle of these common insects. Next time you see a kangaroo paw flower lacking anthers, try looking around in the undergrowth. You might find a skinny, flightless, stick-like grasshopper recovering from a nocturnal banquet.

Honey bees after nectar and pollen

Where the bee sucks . . .

The European honey bee *Apis mellifera* is occasionally seen thieving nectar from species such as *A. manglesii* and *Macropidia*. Such activity does not result in pollination because the anthers and stigma are well separated from the nectar store in these species. Only when honey bees gather pollen is there a chance that stigmas will be brushed and pollination occur.

Near Jurien, Elisabeth Brown (a Masters student from Curtin University of Technology) observed that honey bees were frequent visitors of the flowers of *A. pulcherrimus*. They mainly harvested pollen in the morning, and nectar in the early afternoon. The fact that *A. pulcherrimus* has small flowers meant that honey bees frequently contacted anthers and stigmas while pushing down the throat of the perianth after nectar. However, they were often seen opportunistically to rob nectar through holes slashed in the side of the perianth by birds, in which case no pollination occurred. The honey bees usually visited flowers on adjacent stems on the same plant. Hence, their feeding behaviour is likely to result in higher levels of self-pollination than that of the honeyeaters, which are the main native pollinators.

Short-billed nectar thieves

The holes through which the honey bees were able to thieve nectar from *A. pulcherrimus* were probably made by silvereyes, or possibly by weebills, both of which Elisabeth Brown observed on flowering stems near Jurien. Silvereyes have also been seen at Hillman, slashing holes in the base of *A. manglesii* flowers to get at nectar, which is otherwise inaccessible to them because of their short bills and the tightly tubular perianth base. They also caused damage to cultivated kangaroo paws at the Perth Zoo for many years.

Grazing kangaroos

In some circumstances, kangaroos graze kangaroo paw inflorescences and cause substantial damage. In 1986, Elisabeth Brown found that 50% of shooting flower stems of *Macropidia* near Lesueur National Park were grazed by western grey kangaroos (see page 143). The kangaroos grazed stems indiscriminately, from those newly emergent from the leaf fan, to inflorescences in bud and those with newly opened flowers — in fact, wherever there was any soft tissue. Actively growing stems responded to such grazing by sprouting new stems from axillary buds, or from basal leaf fans.

Kangaroos also grazed *A. pulcherrimus*, but to a lesser extent. Elisabeth Brown observed that "Kangaroos appeared to do more damage by treading on culms and knocking stems over in passing, rather than actually grazing them". Kangaroos have been a major problem on wildflower farms near Moore River, where they graze leaves of *A. manglesii* in autumn and early winter, but rarely eat flowers.

Silvereyes slash holes to steal nectar

Although clumsy kangaroos may damage kangaroo paws, Elisabeth Brown found that commercial wildflower pickers removed more stems than did kangaroos at one of her study sites. They took 50–75% of the stems, and no re-sprouting occurred because the entire scape was removed, taking with it all axillary buds.

Further reading

Brown, E. (1988). *Pollination and Seed Production in Two Species of Kangaroo Paws,* Anigozanthos pulcherrimus *and* Macropidia fuliginosa. MAppSc thesis (Curtin University of Technology, Perth).

Gwynne, D.T. and Bailey, W.J. (1988). Mating system, mate choice and ultrasonic calling in a Zaprochiline Katydid (Orthoptera: Tettigoniidae). *Behaviour* **105**, 203–223.

Gwynne, D.T. and Simmons, L.W. (1988). Experimental reversal of courtship roles in an insect. *Nature* **346**, 172–174.

Simmons, L.W. and Bailey, W.J. (1990). Resource influenced sex roles of Zaprochiline Tettigoniids (Orthoptera: Tettigoniidae). *Evolution* **44**, 1853–1868.

What the katydid

Katydids, flightless long-horned grasshoppers, commonly feed on kangaroo paw pollen. Here, one approaches the stamens of a red and green kangaroo paw flower for a nocturnal banquet (large). The other is a female of a smaller species, who has tucked her tail between her legs to eat the nutrient-rich protein mass covering a sperm bundle from a recent mating.

Hybrid characteristics

A rare hybrid (centre) of *A. humilis* (left) and *A. manglesii* (right) shows characteristics intermediate between those of its parents. Note in particular the arrangement of the stamens in the perianth. See also page 97 for a colour photo of these plants.

Mixed marriages: natural hybridisation

Pollination can be a haphazard process, and fickle pollinators sometimes transfer pollen from one kangaroo paw species to another. The outcome varies, from little more than clogging stigmas with unwanted pollen, to successful fertilisation, the production of natural hybrids, and the possible origin of new species.

Hybridisation is a much-overlooked biological phenomenon that can occur when organisms of two different species are crossed. Such matings tend to cause problems during the early stages of embryo development, as the genetic material from the two different parents can be incompatible. Often this proves to be an insurmountable barrier and there are no viable offspring. But in some instances, usually when the parental species are closely related, pollination is successful, and progeny result that are natural hybrids of the two parents.

Recognising hybrids

In the wild, natural hybrids are usually rare, but they do occur in certain situations, and are easily recognised once you know what to look for. There are several tell-tale signs that might indicate whether an unusual specimen is a natural hybrid. Where the preferred habitats of two species overlap, and they grow together in mixed stands, there is a chance that interspecific pollination will occur. In such situations rare hybrids might be found, especially where pollinators are observed moving from one parent species to another.

Hybrids usually have characteristics that are intermediate between those of the parental species. If wild plants have many such intermediate features, and their features are a good match with those of experimentally synthesised hybrids, this is taken by botanists as compelling evidence that they are natural hybrids.

In addition, hybrid plants are often sterile, or partly so. This can be because of irregular pairing of their chromosomes in the formation of pollen or ovules, or other developmental abnormalities such as aborted or mis-shapen seeds.

Where hybrids do produce viable offspring, such progeny normally display quite variable features, often ranging from those seen in one parent right through to those of the other. A final test of a suspected wild hybrid is therefore to attempt to germinate seed and raise the progeny, to check whether they display variable characteristics (see page 53).

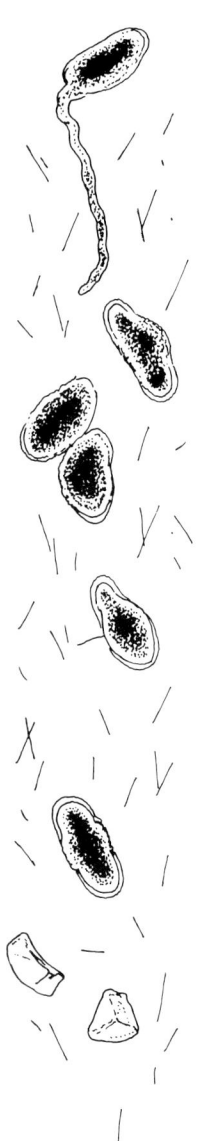

Calcium oxalate needles and pollen grains. Germinating (top) and sterile (bottom)

Hybridisation

Hybrids seem to be a lot more common among plants than among some animals. They are very rare among the larger mammals and birds, partly because their mechanisms of sexual reproduction and development are very complicated. Mixing incompatible chromosomes together in a hybrid is likely to disrupt such processes, and hybrid offspring are unlikely to occur. In contrast, plants have much simpler developmental and sexual processes, and hybridisation is more commonly successful. In addition, mammals and birds are mobile and have an amazing repertoire of behavioural tricks to ensure that they mate with the right individual. Plants, being immobile, are necessarily passive players in the mating game, and usually have to rely on other agents to transfer pollen between them.

As we have seen in Chapter 6, plants such as the kangaroo paws can influence the behaviour of their pollinators to some extent by altering the timing and volume of nectar production. But such devices cannot guarantee faithful pollination. Inevitably, the pollen placed on stigmas will sometimes come from another species. Among plant genera, there are a range of different responses to pollination by other species. Some plants (for example, the triggerplants *Stylidium* spp.) adhere strictly to their own species, and powerful genetic mechanisms operate to ensure that foreign pollen does not waste ovules by producing sickly hybrid seed or offspring. Other genera (for example, some eucalypts and orchids) are more genetically tolerant, and interspecific pollination is less rigorously avoided. Robust hybrids are occasionally produced, some of which may start breeding true themselves and become new species in their own right. Indeed, some botanists now suggest that new plant species are formed by this means much more commonly than had been suspected previously.

Hybrid kangaroo paws

The kangaroo paws and catspaws exhibit a full range of responses to natural interspecific pollination. At one extreme, natural hybrids between *Macropidia* and any species of *Anigozanthos* have never been seen, and no one has ever produced a synthesised hybrid of these two genera, despite determined efforts by several experimental hybridists. There seem to be powerful genetic barriers preventing the formation of intergeneric hybrid seed.

Within the *Anigozanthos* genus, there are some species that are frequently found growing together, and yet never seem to produce a natural hybrid. This usually seems to be the case where a single-stemmed species such as *A. humilis* grows together with a branching-stemmed species such as *A. pulcherrimus* or *A. rufus*. Very rarely, solitary, highly sterile hybrids of single-stemmed and branching-stemmed species have been found: for example, *A. flavidus x viridis* (a hybrid between *A. flavidus* and *A. viridis*) from the Scott River plains, and *A. gabrieliae x rufus* from the Stirling Range foothills.

Natural hybrids are more commonly encountered when different single-stemmed species grow together (although the single-stemmed catspaw *A. humilis* and the branched catspaw *A. onycis* also hybridise quite frequently). If the parental species differ in many features (for example, *A. humilis* and *A. manglesii* or *A. viridis*), the hybrids are rare and usually sterile. But where the parents are similar (for example, *A. bicolor* and *A. viridis*), they are much more common, and will sometimes dominate a population. Perhaps the most common of all is the hybrid of *A. manglesii x viridis*, the plant described by the botanist Dr John Lindley in 1837 as *A. manglesii* var. *angustifolius* (Chapter 10).

Careful ecological studies show that despite the prevalence of hybrids at some sites, they are usually confined to small areas of intermediate habitat linking the habitats preferred by the parental species. For example, hybrids of *A. manglesii x viridis* occur at the junction of winter-wet swamps and flats favoured by *A. viridis*, and surrounding sandy rises occupied by *A. manglesii*.

A fertile population of hybrids, once established, might be expected to spread from the intermediate habitat into the habitats of the parental species, but this does not seem to occur. The mechanisms that confine hybrids to such intermediate habitats have been investigated using the population of *A. humilis*, *A. manglesii* and their hybrids at Gingin cemetery. One possibility is that the hybrids are less fit than the parental species, and are unable to compete with the parental species in their favoured habitats. But in experimental pot trials, the hybrids are every bit as vigorous as *A. manglesii* and actually do better than *A. humilis*. Alternatively, hybrids may be confined to intermediate habitats because movement of pollen between species by honeyeaters only occurs where they grow immediately side by side. As with many deceptively simple ecological observations, the factors determining the confined distribution of hybrids are likely to prove complex.

We do not know whether any of the extant kangaroo paw species originated as hybrids, but *A. kalbarriensis* may have done so. It grows with or near *A. humilis* and *A. manglesii* near Kalbarri, and has several features that match those of some hybrids of these two species from the Gingin cemetery. In recent years, powerful biochemical tools have been developed that allow the genetic material (DNA) of plants to be studied and compared. In the same way that 'DNA fingerprinting' is used to resolve paternity disputes in humans, these techniques could provide clues as to the origin of *A. kalbarriensis*.

Further reading

Grant, V (1981). *Plant Speciation*. 2nd edn. (Colombia University Press, New York.)

Hopper, S.D. (1977). The structure and dynamics of a hybrid population of *Anigozanthos manglesii* D. Don and *A. humilis* Lindl. *Australian Journal of Botany* **25**, 413–422.

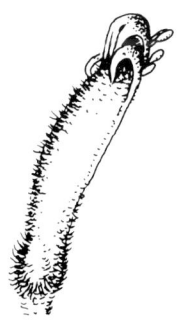

A. kalbarriensis

Hopper, S.D. (1977). The reproductive capacity of *Anigozanthos manglesii* D. Don, *A. humilis* Lindl. and their hybrids in a wild population. *Australian Journal of Botany* **25**, 423–428.

Hopper, S.D. (1978). Progeny trials in an introgressive hybrid population of *Anigozanthos* Labill. (Haemodoraceae). *Australian Journal of Botany* **26**, 309–317.

Hopper, S.D. (1978). An experimental study of competitive interference between *Anigozanthos manglesii* D. Don, *A. humilis* Lindl. and their hybrids (Haemodoraceae). *Australian Journal Botany* **26**, 807–817.

Hopper, S.D. (1978). *Speciation in the Kangaroo Paws of South-western Australia (Anigozanthos and* Macropidia: *Haemodoraceae)*. PhD thesis (The University of Western Australia, Perth).

Hopper, S.D. and Burbidge, A.H. (1978). Assortative pollination by red wattlebirds in a hybrid population of *Anigozanthos* Labill. (Haemodoraceae). *Australian Journal of Botany* **26**, 335–350.

Hybrids produce variable offspring

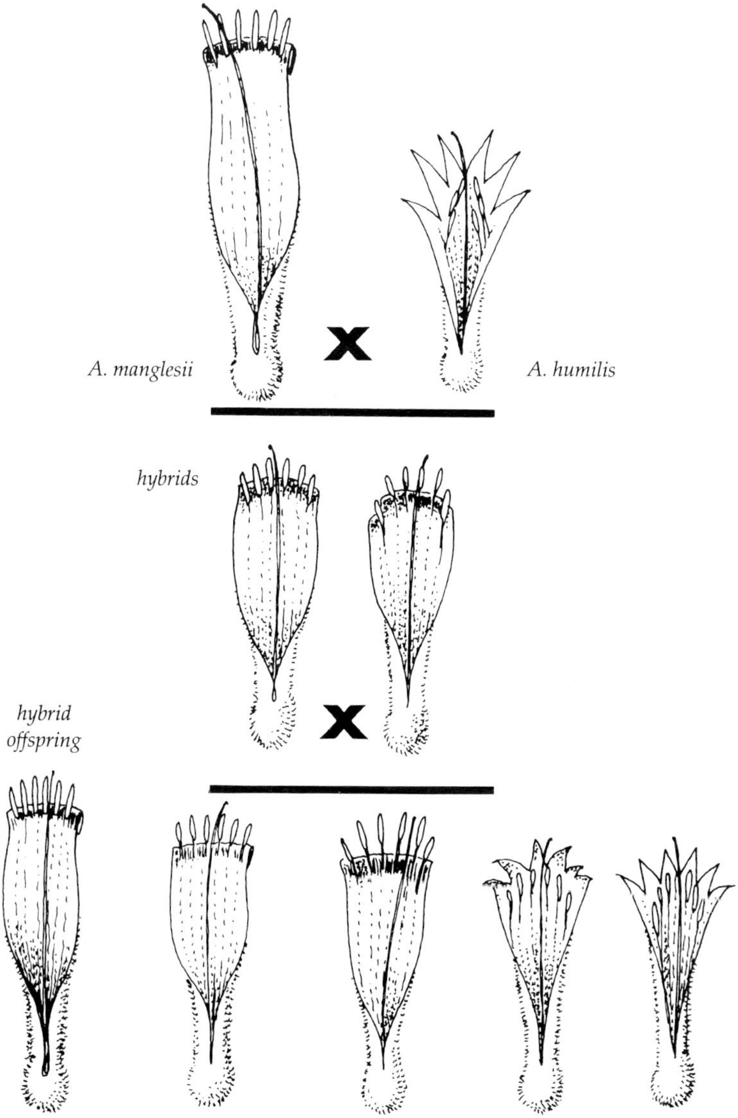

A. manglesii ✕ *A. humilis*

hybrids

✕

hybrid offspring

A good way to test whether a plant is a natural hybrid, is to gather its seeds and germinate them. If the plant is indeed a hybrid, the resultant offspring will be highly variable. Some may closely resemble the parents, but many will have features that are intermediate between those of the two parents. By contrast, the offspring of plants of the same species are much more uniform. This is illustrated here by the perianths of *A. manglesii*, *A. humilis* and their natural hybrids.

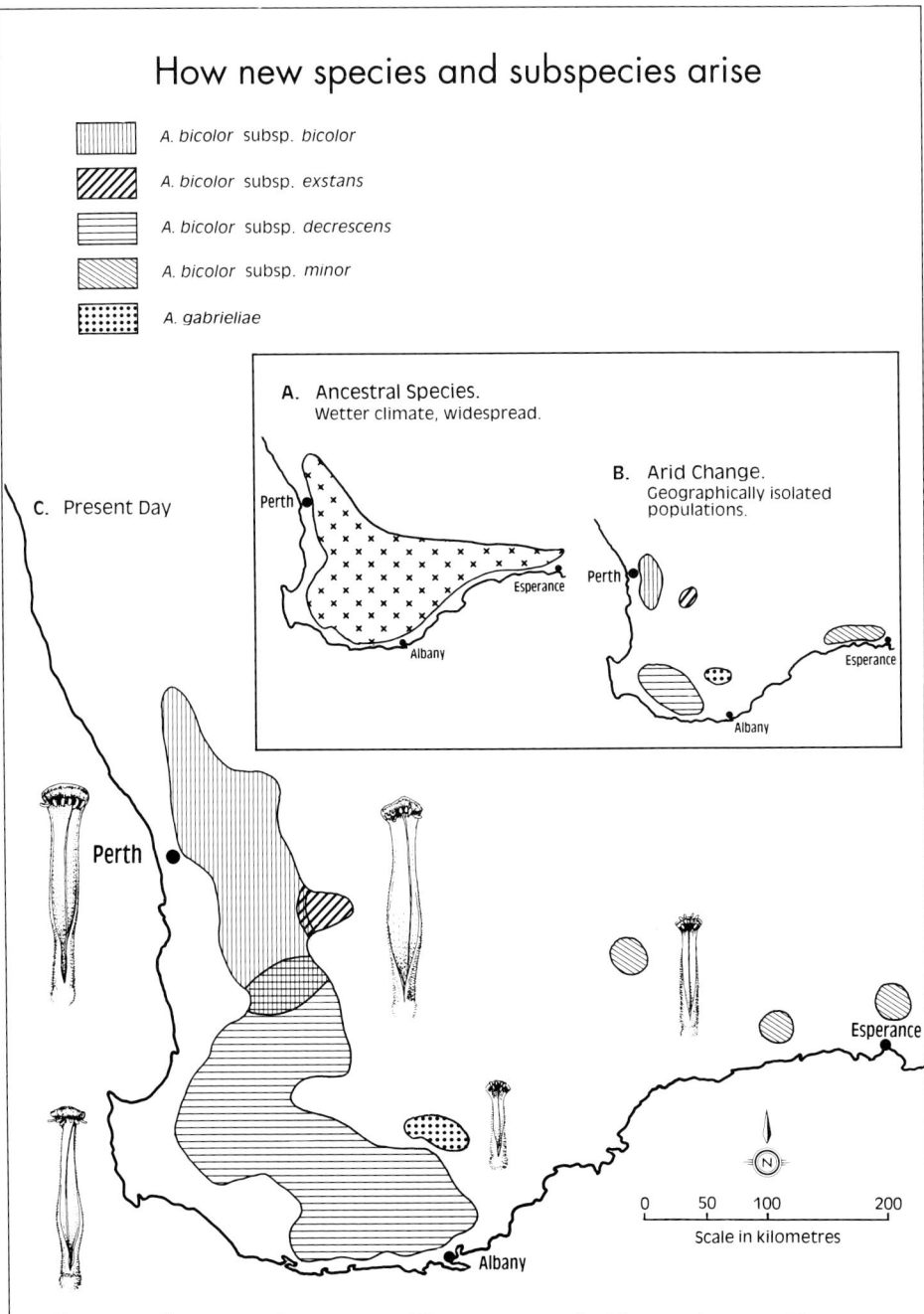

Changes in climate over the past two million years caused widespread ancestral kangaroo paw species (A) to form isolated populations (B), which subsequently evolved into the different species and subspecies that we know today (C).

A family history

When we look at the rich variety of kangaroo paws in the south-west, we may well wonder how there came to be so many species. The features that characterise individual species can offer many clues as to the process of evolution that formed them.

The idea that animal and plant species were not simply created, but have gradually evolved over millions of years from some simple common ancestor, is now widely accepted. The exciting discoveries in Africa of the fossil remains of our own australopithecine ancestors is but one of many pieces of evidence supporting the view that evolution underpins all biological life. This process of evolution was best illuminated by Charles Darwin, when he published his theory of evolutionary change by natural selection in *The Origin of Species* in 1859.

Darwin's theory was simply that variation exists among individuals in all populations, and those individuals with inherited features best suited to a given environment will produce more surviving offspring than those with less appropriate features. Thus, natural selection means that such advantageous features will become dominant in the population as generations turn over. His model of evolutionary change by natural selection is now supported by such a large body of evidence, acquired by so many independent investigators, that it has become one of the central accepted principles of modern biological science.

But evolution is usually by its nature a very slow process. How can we study a process that takes many generations to occur? Where ancient plants and animals have been preserved in fossil form, they can provide clues as to what the forebears of our modern plants and animals looked like. But there are no known fossils of the kangaroo paws. How then is it possible to learn about their evolution?

Charles Darwin's major contribution was to show that careful study of patterns of variation and breeding relationships in living organisms can illuminate the evolutionary process.

A question of heritability

A first step in a study of evolutionary relationships is to establish that the variable features studied are actually genetically determined, and are not merely altered because of the environment. The best way to do this is to grow plants in a uniform environment (a glasshouse or common garden). Any differences in such plants must be genetically determined, and therefore heritable.

In the kangaroo paws, glasshouse experiments have shown that features such as the number of flowering stems produced per plant can alter dramatically with environmental conditions in most species. In *A. flavidus*, for example, plants grown in the glasshouse can produce up to 10 times the number of stems seen on plants in the wild. Hence this feature has what is termed low heritability — it is not strongly genetically determined. Such a feature is of little value for unravelling evolutionary relationships (but of great economic importance to commercial cut-flower growers!).

In contrast, the floral features of all species have high heritability. Take, for example, the perianth characteristics that distinguish the two subspecies of *A. manglesii*. *A. manglesii* subsp. *manglesii* always has brilliant red stems and ovaries, with the red colour stopping at the base of the perianth. Its perianth is parallel-sided just below the stamens. *A. manglesii* subsp. *quadrans* always has a paler, more orange–red coloration that extends up to a quarter of the way up the perianth. It is noticeably constricted in perianth width below the stamens. These characters are extremely consistent, even when the subspecies are grown in the glasshouse together. Furthermore, synthesised hybrids of the two subspecies are intermediate in these characters. This indicates that many genes are involved, and that they are inherited additively in the hybrid, producing blended floral characters.

Thus, we have convincing evidence that the floral differences of these two subspecies are inherited, and do not occur simply because of peculiarities of the soil or climate in the different habitats occupied by *quadrans* and *manglesii*.

Similar evidence exists for the strong heritability of floral features of other kangaroo paw subspecies, such as those of *A. humilis* and *A. bicolor*. It has also been established through experimental hybridisation and glasshouse trials for many of the differences characterising species of *Anigozanthos*.

Natural selection in progress

One of the easiest characteristics to measure in plants is the height of the flowering stems. In the case of the kangaroo paws, it seems probable that the ancestral populations had short flowering stems, as are found in all 46 species of the closely related genus *Conostylis*. How did the taller species of kangaroo paws arise?

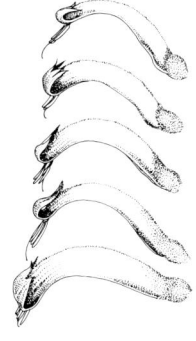

Perianths of A. manglesii *subsp.* manglesii *(top two)*, A. manglesii *subsp.* quadrans *(bottom two) and their synthesised hybrid*

In any population of kangaroo paws, individuals vary in height. Imagine if one of the ancestral populations grew in a habitat where the only pollinators were small furtive honeyeaters wary of feeding close to the ground. Those few unusually tall kangaroo paw plants present might be the only ones pollinated in such circumstances (see Chapter 6). If so, they would contribute many more seeds to the next generation than their shorter, more common, neighbours. Provided flowering stem height was at least partly genetically determined, and not just due to local environmental conditions, the average height of the population would become greater with each generation, until such time as most plants received equivalent pollination, when it would stabilise (see page 59). This is a model of evolutionary change that could be readily tested.

Although a detailed study of such a process in the kangaroo paws has not been undertaken, there is evidence to support the idea that the taller kangaroo paws might have evolved from a shorter ancestor in this way. Stem height is a sufficiently consistent feature that it can be used to distinguish subspecies or species, but variation in flowering stem height has been documented within many wild populations of several species. In experiments, wild plants of different heights were transplanted to a common garden, and their progeny examined. The progeny were found to be of different heights, establishing that differences in stem height are genetically determined, rather than due to the environment, at least for the major height differences characterising subspecies and species. For example, *A. manglesii* always grows taller than *A. humilis* subsp. *humilis* in the garden, and *A. viridis* subsp. *viridis* always grows taller than *A. viridis* subsp. *terraspectans*, although there is still some variation in height within each subspecies.

The question of whether taller plants set more seed than shorter ones within the same species has not been addressed. But we do know that among the group of species that are single-stemmed, the taller species and subspecies set more seed than do the shorter ones.

These observations and experiments lend credence to the notion that evolution by natural selection has indeed occurred in the kangaroo paws.

Evolutionary relationships

Having sorted out genetically determined features from those that are environmentally determined, it is then possible to examine the paths by which the modern species of kangaroo paws evolved, and precisely how they are related.

As populations proceed down separate evolutionary pathways, they accumulate genetic differences through time. Some such differences might arise rapidly under intense natural selection, others more slowly. And some differences might disappear because of convergent evolution under similar selection pressures, or following natural hybridisation. But if a wide enough sample of genetic differences is examined, a key is provided to the evolutionary relationships in a group of plants.

There are so many genetic features available for study that computers have been used to help in looking at patterns and relationships. In addition to features of the plant and flowers, experimental cross-pollination between species provides an indication of how closely they are related. For example, when close relatives are crossed, they would be expected to set high numbers of seeds, and produce some hybrid offspring. Distant relatives that are genetically quite different would not be so compatible, and would be unable to produce so much viable seed (see Chapter 8).

Other characters found by studying the ecology of species in the wild may provide clues as to relationships between species. Soil-type and moisture preferences, flowering times, and the ability to produce natural hybrids, all add to understanding of genetic similarities and differences.

The accumulated store of such knowledge has enabled the construction of models as to how the kangaroo paws have diverged through time. Three independent studies of this process have been completed, all using computers as an aid in analysing the data.

There is general agreement that an early development in the history of the kangaroo paws was the separation of the single-stemmed species from the branched-stemmed species. Also, the single-stemmed species seem to have evolved and formed new species more than the branched species in recent times.

There is still some argument over *Macropidia*. It remains a matter for debate and further research as to whether the ancestors of *Macropidia* diverged first from those of all other species (now placed in the genus *Anigozanthos*), or whether this occurred after the major split of the kangaroo paws into branched versus single-stemmed lineages.

The most recent evolutionary events in the group were probably the divergence of subspecies in *A. bicolor, A. humilis, A. viridis* and *A. manglesii*. It is likely that some very similar species also evolved fairly recently, given the evidence that we now have for their close genetic relationships (for example, *A. pulcherrimus* and *A. rufus, A. bicolor* and *A. gabrieliae*, and *A. humilis* and *A. kalbarriensis*).

How do new species arise?

Studies on the kangaroo paws have shed light on why the flora of south-western Australia is so unusually rich in species.

The most widely accepted model for the mechanisms by which new species arise is one called 'geographical speciation'. This proposes that geographical isolation is of central importance to the evolution of new species.

If a large population is spread over a wide area, environmental selection pressures are unlikely to cause the genetic make-up of the whole population to change. Thus, even if the environment changes in one part of the range and local variant plants arise there, because they continue to interbreed with the larger population, the variant genes would be swamped by those of the rest of the population.

However, if a small group of plants at the margins of a large population were isolated by, say, the formation of a mountain range, they would face new local

Evolution of flowering stem height

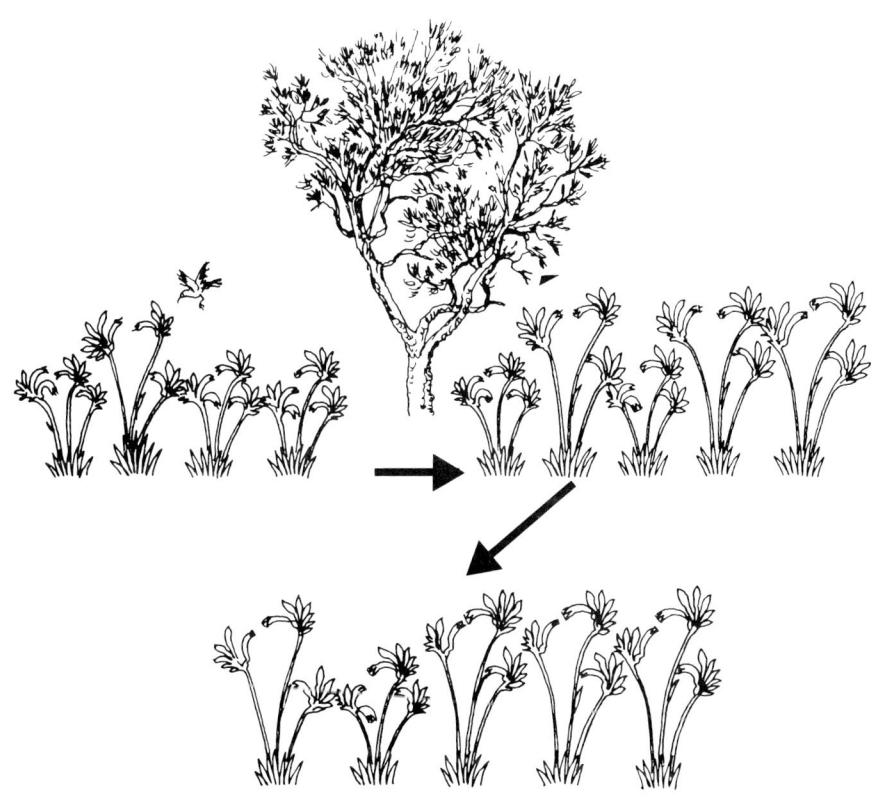

The behaviour of pollinators may be one of the forces for evolutionary change in the kangaroo paws. Where furtive birds that prefer to perch while feeding rather than stand on the ground are the main pollinators, taller plants will receive more attention. Under these circumstances, the taller plants will set more seed and contribute more offspring to succeeding generations. Thus, the population will evolve from mostly short plants to mostly tall plants.

Environmental factors driving speciation

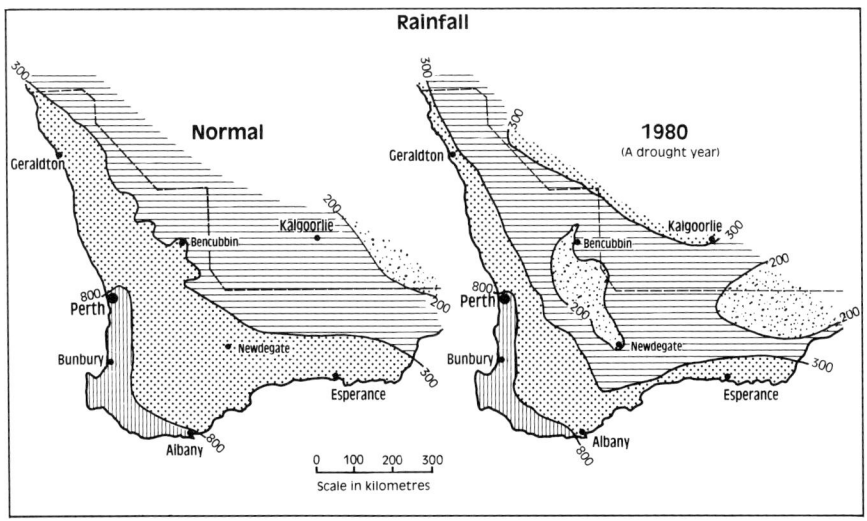

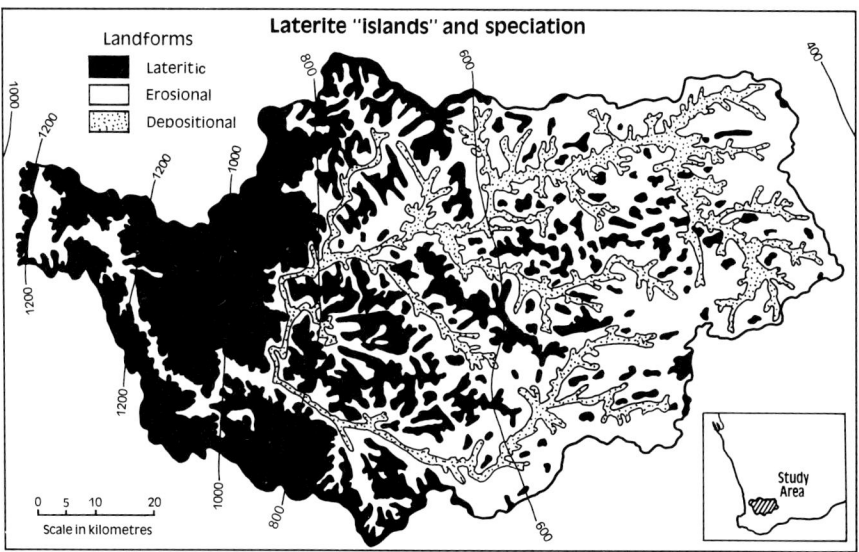

Rainfall distribution in the south-west in a normal year compared with a drought year (top). Note how the most dramatic difference in rainfall coincides with the species-rich wheatbelt. Distribution of lateritic, erosional and depositional areas in the Murray River catchment (bottom). The archipelago of laterite remnants at the eastern end of the catchment coincides with the areas of greatest plant speciation (adapted from McArthur et al., 1977).

selection pressures quite different to those acting on the main parent population. If appropriate genetic variation occurs in the isolated plants, new variant genes might evolve. Their isolation and small number would greatly increase the probability of such new adaptations spreading to all members of the population. The swamping of the new variants by incoming genes that is seen in large populations would not occur.

If in this process, features that restrict interbreeding with the parent population are accidental by-products of some genetic variation, a new species will have arisen. Eventually, with changing climate or landscape evolution, the divergent isolated population might expand its range and be able to grow intermixed with the parent population without interbreeding.

If the geographic speciation model applies to kangaroo paws, you would expect to find subspecies in isolated geographical areas rather than growing close together. You would also expect species that hybridise readily with one another to occupy different geographical ranges (reflecting their recent divergence in isolation), whereas those that diverged longer ago, and were therefore genetically more different, would have stronger barriers to hybridisation and might more often grow together.

The kangaroo paws do indeed show such distribution patterns. We see isolated races or subspecies well separated from the main species' range (for example, the eastern race subsp. *minor* of *A. bicolor*). *A. bicolor* ranges from the Moore River to Albany and Esperance, but its close relative *A. gabrieliae* is confined to an isolated population in the Stirling Range (see page 54). *A. rufus* and *A. pulcherrimus* are well-separated species that are closely related. In both these cases, artificial hybridisation in the glasshouse yields fairly fertile hybrids, indicating that the species have evolved relatively recently from a common ancestor. There are several geographically distinct races or subspecies that merge or intergrade where their ranges overlap (for example, subspecies in *A. manglesii, A. bicolor, A. viridis* and *A. humilis*). The hybrid plants of different subspecies in such populations are usually fertile.

There are many cases of more distantly related species that overlap in distribution and produce partly sterile hybrids, as discussed in Chapter 8 (for example, *A. manglesii* and *A. humilis*). And there are very distinct species that grow together and produce no natural hybrids at all (for example, *A. humilis* and *A. pulcherrimus*).

On this evidence, it seems that most of the kangaroo paw species could have arisen by geographic speciation, but more work is needed to test these ideas.

Origins of the rich south-western flora

Regardless of the mechanisms by which new kangaroo paw species and subspecies evolved, it is interesting to note that the process has clearly not been random throughout the south-west. Rather, recently evolved kangaroo paws are concentrated in two areas — the western heathlands to the north of Perth, and the southern heathlands near the Stirling Range–Albany district. The species found in the intervening high-rainfall forests (for example, *A. flavidus*) display much less genetic variation. The same is true for many plant groups, particularly woody genera such as the one-sided bottlebrushes (*Calothamnus*), the feather flowers (*Verticordia*), *Grevillea* and *Hakea*. Why is this so?

Something special in the northern and southern heathlands has caused fragmentation and isolation of plant populations, promoting evolutionary divergence and the formation of new species. This force has not been as active in the forests, at least not for groups like the kangaroo paws.

The evolutionary pressure in the heathlands seems to have come from a combination of two different factors: climatic fluctuations during the past two million years or more, and a complex mosaic of rapidly eroding soil types (see page 60).

Much of the present-day heathland terrain of the south-west was covered in luxuriant subtropical rainforest for many millions of years, until the drifting apart of Australia from Antarctica set in train a change to a more arid climate. Under the subtropical conditions, lateritic gravel soils had been formed, but the onset of aridity largely stopped this and led to progressive erosion of the lateritised landscape.

More resistant or thicker pockets of laterite have persisted to the present day as the familiar flat-topped mesas and breakaways of the heathland and wheatbelt areas (for example, Mt Lesueur). These are now like 'islands' surrounded by sandplains and valleys. Plant communities that once occurred in the rainforests throughout the region were fragmented into innumerable smaller populations on the 'islands' of residual laterite. Those plants preferring to grow on erosional sands were able to establish themselves on the new heathlands in between.

Pronounced shifts of climatic zones during the ice ages of the past two million years have driven this dramatic change in the distribution of soil types. These shifts from dry, cold conditions to wetter, warmer ones would also have altered the ranges of plant populations.

The fact that lateritic soils persist to the present day in the high-rainfall forests, together with many relic plants and animals with subtropical affinities, indicate that the forests of the south-west did not experience such dramatic climatic fluctuations or soil erosion as the heathlands, or the areas near the coast, where sea levels waxed and waned. This explains why speciation in the forests has been much less pronounced than in the heathlands.

In the forests we see *A. flavidus*, the species with primitive evergreen leaves and flowers that are closest to those of the closely related genus *Conostylis*. Essentially, this species occupies habitats not far removed from the ancestral subtropical rainforests that once dominated the south-west. It is a vigorous relic species that has not been subjected to much pressure for change.

At the other extreme, occupying the highly seasonal and fire-prone heathlands, are several species showing extensive geographical variation, advanced floral features and vegetative growth adapted to the seasonality of a mediterranean climate (for example, *A. humilis*, *A. manglesii*, *A. bicolor*). These are the outcome of the most recent and explosive evolutionary episode in the history of the kangaroo paws.

Further reading

Anderberg, A.A. and Eldenas, P. (1991). A cladistic study of *Anigozanthos* and *Macropidia*. *Australian Systematic Botany* **4**, 655–664.

Darwin, C. (1859). *The Origin of Species*. (London.)

Grant, V. (1981). *Plant Speciation*. 2nd edn. (Columbia University Press, New York.)

Hopper, S.D. (1978). *Speciation in the Kangaroo Paws of South-western Australia (Anigozanthos and Macropidia: Haemodoraceae)*. PhD thesis (The University of Western Australia, Perth).

Hopper, S.D. (1979). Biogeographical aspects of speciation in the south west Australian flora. *Annual Review of Ecology and Systematics* **10**, 399–422.

Hopper, S.D. (1980). A biosystematic study of the kangaroo paws, *Anigozanthos* and *Macropidia* (Haemodoraceae). *Australian Journal of Botany* **28**, 659–80.

Hopper, S.D. and Campbell, N.A. (1977). A multivariate morphometric study of species relationships in kangaroo paws (*Anigozanthos* Labill. and *Macropidia* Drumm. ex Harv.: Haemodoraceae). *Australian Journal of Botany* **25**, 523–544.

James, S.H. and Hopper, S.D. (1981). Speciation in the Australian flora. In J.S. Pate and A.J. McComb (eds), *The Biology of Australian Plants*, pp. 361–381. (University of Western Australia Press, Perth.)

McArthur, W.M., Churchward, H.M. and Hick, P.T. (1977). Landforms and soils of the Murray River catchment area of Western Australia. *CSIRO Australian Division of Land Resource Management*, **3**, 1–23.

Pioneering botanists

The names that we use today for the kangaroo paws have evolved out of a rich tradition of botanical endeavour, involving a diverse range of late eighteenth and nineteenth century European explorers and scientists, and colonial collectors, as well as modern contributors.

After at least 40 000 years of living in the south-west of Western Australia, the Aborigines must have had a rich and varied store of knowledge about the kangaroo paws and their uses. Regrettably, such Aboriginal knowledge is poorly documented. All that has been recorded is that the evergreen kangaroo paw *A. flavidus* was called *cattech, cathah* or *cassiteh* and *koroylbardang*, and the Aborigines apparently used the rhizomes of young plants that had not yet flowered for food. The red and green kangaroo paw *A. manglesii* was known as *kuttych, kurulbrang* or *krulbrang*.

The story of the discovery and naming of the kangaroo paws by botanists of European descent stretches over two centuries, and provides an intriguing insight into the cut and thrust of botanical naming. The discovery of a new plant species is only the first step in bringing it to the attention of other botanists throughout the world. One must then convincingly demonstrate that it is indeed a new species, and not simply a subtle variant of a species that has already been documented and named. Only then may one claim the honour of choosing the name by which it shall be known. But the naming of species is an emotive subject, and has inspired some heated debates. Many an intrepid early naturalist, keen to 'plant his flag' on a new species, has had that pleasure snatched from him by a more assiduous rival.

European scientific collectors

The Frenchman Jacques J.H. de Labillardière was naturalist on Admiral Bruny d'Entrecasteaux's expedition to Australia during 1791–94. He collected some 4 000 plant specimens, as well as mammals, reptiles, birds and fish. Over the period 9–17 December 1792, the expedition sought refuge from a storm, repaired the rudder bars of the ship *Espérance*, and searched for fresh water supplies near the modern town of Esperance on Western Australia's south coast. Here Labillardière encountered the rich burgundy-coloured plant he was later to name *Anigozanthos rufus*.

It is not certain that Labillardière himself collected specimens of the plant. A number of landings were made by different parties, some sent in search of the doctor and botanist Charles Riche, who became lost inland from Dempster Head on 15 December. The next day Riche abandoned the plant specimens he had collected, in his urgency to get back to the coast before the ships departed. Possibly Labillardière or another collector found the striking

J.J.H. de Labillardière, (1755–1834) the first botanist to name a kangaroo paw

kangaroo paw while searching for Riche. In any event, at least one specimen was collected and survives to this day in the Paris Herbarium.

Bringing the discoveries of the expedition to the attention of European science was not a straightforward matter. Because France had recently declared war on the Dutch, the unsuspecting members of the expedition were held in Java on their return voyage in 1793–94. Their collections were confiscated and sent to Britain. But after the diplomatic negotiations of Sir Joseph Banks, the plant collections were eventually returned to Labillardière, who had made his way back to Paris, and he was then able to describe the many new species collected by the expedition. He named *A. rufus* in 1798, the first kangaroo paw to be named by a European botanist.

The name that Labillardière chose for his burgundy kangaroo paw was almost as tortuous in its derivation as the path followed by his collections back to Paris from Australia. After much debate, botanists now generally agree that Labillardière coined *Anigozanthos* from the Greek *anisos* (unequal) and *anthos* (flower), alluding to the unequal lobes of the perianth, with the *g* and the *z* inserted for euphony. (There is also general agreement that *Anigozanthos* is the correct spelling, although other spellings have been used in some previous publications.)

Thus, recorded knowledge of *Anigozanthos* has its origin in the bold initiatives of French scientific exploration of the southern Australian coastline. As with many scientific discoveries, a combination of serendipity, luck and diligence placed Labillardière in the position of describing as new to the western world, the first of this remarkable group of plants. His discovery arose in circumstances typical of those faced by Europeans in contact with this strange new land — sheltering from a storm, seeking meagre supplies of water at the start of a hot dry summer, and in search of a colleague lost in the bush.

Aware of French activity in the region, the British moved quickly to commission a major exploratory expedition of Australia, which was led by Captain Matthew Flinders on the *Investigator*. The ship anchored at King George Sound (Albany) on 8 December 1801. On board as naturalist was a young Scot, Robert Brown, appointed under the patronage of Sir Joseph Banks. Also in the party were the gardener Peter Good, as conservator, and the artist Ferdinand Bauer.

Robert Brown (1773–1858)

A full month (until 5 January 1802) was spent in the Sound, affording Brown, Good and others ample opportunity to explore and collect plants from a range of habitats around Albany. They encountered and collected the evergreen kangaroo paw in full flower over this period, as it was, and still is, very common in the district. But Brown, destined to become known as the father of Australian botany, was pre-empted from describing the evergreen kangaroo paw as new by another French party, as he did not publish his book describing the expedition's collections until 1810. Brown also collected *A. rufus* at Lucky Bay east of Esperance as the *Investigator* made towards Sydney.

Record of a pioneering era

The original specimen of *A. rufus* collected by Labillardière in 1792 near the present-day town of Esperance. The specimen is still stored in the Paris Herbarium. (T.D. Macfarlane)

Portrait of Captain Mangles

Captain James Mangles (1786–1867), the horticultural enthusiast who initiated and supported major collections of the south-west Australian flora by James Drummond and others. *A. manglesii*, the State Floral Emblem of Western Australia, is named after him. Mangles joined the Royal Navy in 1800 and retired about 1816 with the rank of Captain. Widely travelled, and from a family with large shipping interests, Mangles was ideally placed to promote horticultural exploration. He visited the Swan River Colony in 1831 at the request of his cousin, Lady Stirling. He was pivotal for several subsequent years in the distribution of collections, including seed of several kangaroo paws, to nurserymen and botanists in England. His brother, Robert, was a nurseryman in Berkshire, and raised several south-western plants to flowering, including *A. manglesii*.

In February 1803, Thomas Nicholas Baudin's expedition spent a few weeks at King George Sound. The expedition included botanists André Michaud, Leschenault de la Tour and Jacques Delisse, head gardener Anselme Riedlé, and gardener's boys Antoine Guichenot and Antoine Sautier. Baudin, Guichenot and Riedlé are credited with collections of the evergreen kangaroo paw, which were successfully brought back to Paris. From these, the species was named *Anigozanthos flavidus* in 1807 by Augustus P. de Candolle, Professor of Botany at Montpellier.

The British botanist Allan Cunningham, with Phillip Parker King's Australian coastal survey expedition, was at King George Sound during January 1818 and December–January 1822. Because both visits were in summer, he missed collecting the common Albany catspaw in flower. He did, however, make collections of *A. rufus* on the expedition.

The visiting horticultural collector William Baxter failed similarly to bring back surviving specimens of the Albany catspaw during his times at King George Sound in 1823–25 and 1829. The British would again be pre-empted by botanists from elsewhere in naming this catspaw.

The mystery of Mangles' kangaroo paw

Following the establishment of the Swan River Colony (Perth) in 1829, the botany of the south-west was opened up to detailed exploration by visiting natural historians. One was Captain James Mangles, retired naval commander, who for three months in autumn–winter of 1831 visited his cousin Lady Stirling, the Governor's wife. Mangles, a Fellow of the Royal Society and a Fellow of the Royal Geographical Society, was noted for his book *Travels in Egypt, Nubia, Syria and Asia Minor in 1817–18*. He also promoted the growing of species from foreign countries in gardens throughout Britain.

Mangles met many of the Swan River colonists during his stay, and struck up a friendship with George Fletcher Moore, Commissioner of the Civil Court. The timing of Mangles' visit in late autumn to early winter meant that he missed the main wildflower season. However, Moore gave Mangles "some specimens of flowering shrubs, besides a bottle full of snakes, lizards and scorpions" as a gift of Swan River collections. These, together with others taken back to England by Mangles, aroused considerable interest in the exotic flora and fauna of south-western Australia.

It is not clear whether seeds of a striking red and green kangaroo paw were included among the specimens. But seeds of it were certainly brought to England by Governor Stirling, and were germinated and successfully raised in cultivation. The Scottish horticulturist David Don described and illustrated the new species in 1834, naming it *Anigozanthos manglesii* in honour either of Captain Mangles or his brother Robert (who raised the species to flowering in Berkshire), or for both gentlemen.

The description of *A. manglesii* appeared in R. Sweet's *The British Flower Garden, series II*, accompanied by the following description:

"This singularly beautiful species of *Anigozanthos* was raised in the garden at Whitmore Lodge, Berkshire, the seat of Robert Mangles, Esq. from seeds brought from Swan River by Sir James Stirling, the enterprizing governor of that colony, by whom they had been presented to Mr Mangles."

Among Mangles' seeds were certainly a few hybrids of *A. manglesii* and *A. viridis*, the most common natural hybrid found among the kangaroo paws. In 1837 Dr John Lindley, Professor of Botany at London University, Secretary of the Horticultural Society, and renowned orchidologist, named a new narrow-leaved variety *A. manglesii* var. *angustifolius* from seed germinated by James Mangles' brother. This variety is undoubtedly a hybrid, the first of such among the kangaroo paws to be named. In his description of this variety, Lindley commented that it was "obtained like its prototype from Swan River by Mr Mangles". Whether he was referring to James or Robert Mangles is not clear. If James was intended, this statement suggests that Captain Mangles collected the original seed of *A. manglesii* from which the species was described, not Governor Stirling as proposed by David Don. However, in the absence of further information, the exact source will remain a subject of speculation.

In 1838, Lindley described *Anigozanthos flavidus* var. *bicolor*, again raised from seed by Robert Mangles. Lindley distinguished this variety by its scarlet and green flowers "harmoniously blended and softened together", and by its more branched flowering stems than those of typical *A. flavidus*. This is a colourful form of the species, mainly from the Margaret River area.

Seeds of another common species from near Perth had also been brought back to England by Mangles, but this was not described by Lindley from cultivated material until 1840. The common catspaw, *Anigozanthos humilis*, was featured in the first detailed account of the flora of the colony, in which Lindley named many new species familiar to Perth citizens. Lindley was impressed by his new species, remarking:

"... of the well-known genus *Anigozanthus* [sic] there are not only the *A. manglesii* and *flavida* [sic] with their beautiful green and purple varieties, but there is a dwarf species still handsomer than they are, in consequence of the compactness of the flowers and the short neat foliage; this *A. humilis* would be a handsome addition to our gardens."

James Drummond
(1784–1863)

James Drummond and Georgiana Molloy — colonial collectors

In July 1835, George Moore and Lady Stirling received letters from Captain Mangles seeking assistance in obtaining further seeds and live plants from Western Australia. Moore was aware that James Drummond and his son

Johnston, then resident in the Helena Valley, were collecting seeds of native plants for shipment and sale at Capetown. Moore purchased 100 packets of seeds from the Drummonds and shipped them back to Mangles immediately. Late in 1835 an enthusiastic reply was received requesting more material.

In the meantime, on 18 September 1835, James Drummond wrote independently to Mangles offering to collect seeds and specimens for payment. A sample of seeds of several species was included with Drummond's letter. Mangles forwarded the letter to Dr Lindley at London University, who wrote back to Mangles in December 1836 in favour of the idea:

"I think good Swan River specimens would sell for two pounds per 100 papers, that is the market price for such things. Probably a dozen purchasers at least would be found. But as it is not known how Drummond would prepare the specimens I recommend him to send 2 or 3 sets of 100 or 150 each upon trial. I will take one set. We horticultural people wish for ten pound worth of seeds and bulbs as a venture. Nothing but very handsome things will do, we would rather have a good deal of seed of a very few sorts than a little seed of a good many sorts. If the seed suit us, we may be very good customers."

Mangles responded immediately to Drummond's letter of September 1835 requesting, among other things, all kinds of orchids. Thus began Drummond's career as a major commercial collector of south-western flora.

Mangles also wrote in December 1836 to colonists recommended by Lady Stirling who might collect seeds for sheer interest rather than as a source of income. Included among these were Mrs Georgiana Molloy of Augusta and Captain Richard Meares of Guildford, both of whom agreed to help.

Mrs Molloy, a keen gardener, and her young family took on the task with enthusiasm through the spring of 1837. Specimens were pressed and numbered as each species flowered, and plants watched thereafter (especially by daughters Sabina and Mary) for the fruits to ripen ready for collection of seed. It is highly probable that Mrs Molloy collected seed of the red flowering form of *A. flavidus* that is common in the Margaret River area. Tragically, her infant son John was drowned in November of that year. Overcoming this event, a subsequent sickness and pregnancy, together with the demands of running an isolated colonial household, delayed preparation for shipment of Mrs Molloy's meticulously pressed specimens for another year. But the delay allowed additional specimens from the spring of 1838 to be added, including plants collected by Captain Molloy from the Vasse (Busselton).

On 16 November 1838, Mrs Molloy shipped her specimens and seeds to Lady Stirling for subsequent shipment to Captain Mangles in London. In 1839, horticulturist Joseph Paxton named a new species, *Anigozanthos coccineus*, from Swan River Colony seed cultivated in England by R. Mangles. This was the red flowering form of *A. flavidus*. It is no longer recognised as a species.

Georgiana Molloy (1805–1843)

Thus, Mrs Molloy's diligent efforts were not rewarded by having a lasting name applied to any kangaroo paw that she and her family collected. A later attempt to name a striking new species of kangaroo paw after her posthumously was also to fail.

In 1839 a German botanist, Ludwig Preiss, arrived at the Swan River Colony, and embarked on extensive collecting expeditions, some in company with James Drummond. Although the two men both encountered and collected several new kangaroo paws, it was the collections of Preiss that were used by a botanist back in Germany to name *Anigozanthos bicolor, A. viridis* and *A. preissii* in 1846. These species were named by Stephan L. Endlicher, Professor of Botany and Director of the Botanical Gardens in Vienna, in a treatment of the kangaroo paws collected by Preiss published in the two-volume work *Plantae Preissiana*. In the same work, Endlicher also named a variety (*plumosus*) of *A. preissii*, which is difficult to distinguish from the typical form and is no longer recognised. Another species, *A. minimus*, was named in the same publication by the editor of *Plantae Preissiana*, Johann G.C. Lehmann, Professor of Botany and Director of the Botanical Gardens at Hamburg. Preiss's specimen of *A. minimus* was collected "towards the foot of the Darling Range", and has recently been confirmed to be the same as Lindley's earlier named species *A. humilis*.

Although he was an astute observer and collector of new species of plant, James Drummond was not destined to collect any specimens of kangaroo paws named as new to science (except *A. flavidus* var. *bicolor*, which is no longer recognised today, being merely a colour form common in the Margaret River area -see page 142). He forwarded specimens of *A. bicolor, A. viridis* and *A. preissii* to Lindley and other subscribers in London in 1839 and 1840. But none were taken up and described as new at the time, enabling Endlicher to publish their names six years later.

Drummond nevertheless recorded interesting observations of the kangaroo paws during this exciting period of discovery. Some of his notes in letters to Sir William Hooker, Foundation Director of the Royal Botanic Gardens at Kew, were published in the *London Journal of Botany*. For example, Drummond wrote about different races of *A. humilis* that he had observed, in a letter from Toodyay dated 14 October 1839:

"The cream coloured *Anigozanthos* found between Waylen's Rd and Guangan [now Wongan Hills], seems not distinct from the early orange, or only a form of it, and I have met with another variety of the same species on the downs near the sea, about 10 miles to the north of Freemantle. The three varieties are as follows:-

Sir William Hooker (1785–1865)

a. the early orange, which grows on the sandhills between the Swan River and the Darling Range; this plant springs up singly and is about 9" high, with orange flowers and is the earliest of the genus; it has one or two large leaves near the ground from the axis of which the flowering branches are produced.

b. the sea coast variety attaining about 1' high, a strong plant bearing many flowers; there are 4–5 large leaves on the stems from which flowering branches are produced; the flowers are often yellow or yellow variegated with orange.

c. the cream coloured variety which grows 2' high with 2 or 3 flowery branches from each root; the stems have 2–3 large leaves which produce flowering branches from their axils; the inflorescence is of a beautiful cream colour, but frequently marked with orange near the mouth of the corolla."

Drummond had clearly described the three subspecies now recognised in *A. humilis*, with his a. being subsp. *humilis*, his b. probably subsp. *'grandis'* (the height given, about one foot, is at the low end for this subspecies, and the "sea coast" differs from the inland alluvial sites currently known, but all other characters are a good match), and his c. being subsp. *chrysanthus* (again, the locality given, between Waylen's Rd and Wongan Hills, has not been confirmed by subsequent collectors, possibly due to agricultural clearing, but the description is otherwise accurate for this subspecies, except for the reference to orange floral markings).

Given that Lindley obviously showed some reluctance to distinguish as new species *A. bicolor*, *A. viridis* and *A. preissii* from Drummond's collections, it is perhaps no surprise that he did not take up Drummond's varieties of *A. humilis* either, and publish them as new.

Drummond wrote a later letter to Hooker, dated 13 April 1842, after he had received from England a copy of Lindley's 1840 publication *A Sketch of the Vegetation of the Swan River Colony*, in which only *A. humilis* was described as new. The Scottish collector was obviously perplexed as to why all his other 1839 specimens, separately numbered as distinct new species, had not been taken up by Lindley and described as new. With regard to the kangaroo paws, Drummond wrote:

"126 [his collection number] is a new *Anigozanthos* which grows in the sandy country about 50 miles to the north of this place [Toodyay], it is easily distinguished from *flavida* by its short sickle-shaped hairy leaves. [This was clearly the eastern race of a species later named by Hooker *A. pulcherrimus*.]

"I do not know what Dr. Lindley calls *Anigozanthos manglesii* with its beautiful green and purple variety. If it is our large species the *latifolia* of Frazer our dwarf green and crimson [*A. bicolor*], and our green swamp [*A. viridis*] are certainly very distinct species from it.

"Dr Lindley's *A. humilis* is my early orange, of which I sent account of several varieties. My dwarf green and crimson is the *A. moorii* of Preiss, it nearly agrees with the green swamp *Anigozanthos* in the form of the leaves but they are less glaucous and the species are very distinct. The *A. moorii* of Preiss has a wide range, it is common in the best description of pastoral land from the Swan River to Mount Barker. I have seen it for 300 miles from north to south."

The vastly improved knowledge of kangaroo paws today fully supports Drummond's assessment of the different species and subspecies he had collected. *A. 'moorii'* was never published by Preiss, and the name was not taken up by Endlicher, who chose instead *A. bicolor*.

Interestingly, there is a Preiss collection of *A. bicolor* at the herbarium at Kew, labelled *Anigozanthos 'mooreana' mihi* [of mine], written in Lindley's hand. It would appear that Lindley had entertained naming this species, and intended using a modification of Preiss's proposed name (after George Fletcher Moore). However, Lindley did not publish this name, and it therefore is not accepted nor used today, as *A. bicolor* was the first correctly published name to appear in print. This is regrettable, because Moore did much to foster natural history in the young Swan River Colony, and he recorded a fascinating account of his experiences, particularly with Aborigines, in an 1884 book entitled *Diary of Ten Years Eventful Life of an Early Settler in Western Australia and also A Descriptive Vocabulary of the Language of the Aborigines*.

Although Drummond's collections of new species of kangaroo paws were to languish unacknowledged at Kew, his son Johnston collected two species to the north of Perth which James Drummond was instrumental in shipping to England in January 1843 from his farm at Toodyay. One was golden yellow, a species which Drummond senior had previously sent, and considered it to be "the very loveliest plant which this country can boast". It was named *Anigozanthos pulcherrimus* (Latin for 'most beautiful') by Hooker in 1845. The other, a dark black and green, Drummond himself described in an 1843 letter drafted for the Perth newspaper *The Inquirer*. He intended it to be named *Anigozanthos 'molloyiae'*, after Georgiana Molloy, but the letter was never published. Drummond's manuscript read in part: "*Anigozanthos 'molloyiae'* is a most remarkable plant and it may be said to be a true mourning flower". He therefore wished to dedicate it to "the memory of the lamented lady who is gone to the country from where no botanist returns".

Hooker named the black and green species in 1847 as *Anigozanthos fuliginosus*. Subsequently, it was placed in its own genus, *Macropidia*, in 1855, by Drummond and the British algologist William Harvey (who collected in WA during 1854–56). This marked the end of the pioneering phase of discovery and description of the more common kangaroo paws and catspaws.

Drummond was involved in one further frustrating episode with the naming of kangaroo paws. From Cape Riche on the south coast on 15 January 1847, he wrote to Hooker about a species he encountered while traversing the Kalgan Plains south of the Stirling Range:

"On the way I gathered for the first time a splendid *Anigozanthos* with blood red flowers. From this place we found it common in the sandy valleys all the way to Cape Riche. I named it in complement to my kind friends Mr and Mrs Cheyne *Anigozanthos 'cheyneii'*."

The species was Labillardière's *A. rufus*, of whose identity Drummond was apparently unaware. Moreover, Hooker was similarly mistaken, and published the name *A. tyrianthinus* for the species in 1850. The error was subsequently corrected by George Bentham in 1873 in his monumental *Flora Australiensis: A Description of the Plants of the Australian Territory*.

In 1862, the earliest recorded mention of the common name alluding to a kangaroo paw appeared in *The Floral Magazine*, in an article on *A. manglesii* written by the Reverend H.H. Dombrain. A Mr Kinghorn, of Sheen Nursery, Richmond, had received a special certificate from the Floral Committee of the Royal Horticultural Society for a plant of *A. manglesii* he had grown. Dombrain provided a fine colour plate of this plant, and described its origin as follows:

George Bentham (1800–1884)

"Mr Kinghorn informs us that the seed was presented to him in July of last year by H.W. Pownall, Esq., of Richmond, who received them from his brother, the Very Rev. George P. Pownall, Dean of Perth, Western Australia, labelled 'Anigozanthus, or Kangaroo's-foot plant, the finest we have collected near this city'. He succeeded in raising one plant."

It is probable that the name kangaroo paw was in currency in Perth even earlier (i.e. in the 1850s), because *Macropidia*, named in 1855, is derived from the Greek *macro* (large) and the Latin *pes* (foot) and -*ia* (resembling). Hence the name meant 'resembling the foot of *Macropus*', a genus of kangaroo that includes the common western grey of the south-west.

In 1873, George Bentham named *Anigozanthos bicolor* var. *minor*, a small form of this species, collected by George Maxwell at Culham Inlet near Hopetoun. Bentham also refuted an argument put by Victoria's Government Botanist Ferdinand von Mueller that *Macropidia* should not be retained as a genus distinct from *Anigozanthos*. Bentham stated succinctly: "It [*Macropidia*] is reunited with *Anigozanthos* by F. Mueller, notwithstanding the remarkable differences in the ovary and fruit". This was the first recorded exchange in what has become a perennial debate about the classification of the two genera.

Twentieth century discoveries

Botanical science in Western Australia received a boost in 1897 with the appointment of retired Scottish medical practitioner Dr Alexander Morrison as Botanist with the Bureau (later Department) of Agriculture. Although his job was mainly to assist farmers with the identification of poison plants, weeds and forage species, Morrison collected many other native plants.

In September 1902, Morrison was the first botanist since Drummond to investigate the diverse flora of the Stirling Range. Somewhere east from Solomon's Hill, on the north side of the range, he encountered a diminutive red and green kangaroo paw. The specimens were subsequently sent to Kew

Gardens, but neither recognised as new nor named at the time. In 1910, this same species was collected between Cranbrook and Warrungup (Mt Trio) by the British officer Captain A.A. Dorrien-Smith. His specimens were also taken back to Kew, and subsequently examined and named in 1912 by Karel Domin, Professor of Botany at Prague University. It would seem that Domin did not see Morrison's earlier collection of the dwarf kangaroo paw, because he cited only Dorrien-Smith's specimen when he described *A. gabrieliae* as new. The species was then to languish unrecognised, or confused with *A. bicolor* var. *minor*, until the 1970s.

Domin also named another species, *A. dorrienii*, in the same publication, from material collected by Dorrien-Smith from the same locality as that of *A. gabrieliae*. However, *A. dorrienii* is now regarded merely as a minor variant of *A. humilis* subsp. *humilis*, and is no longer recognised.

A rare yellow-flowered colour form of *A. manglesii* was collected at Kings Park in 1914 by the Danish botanist Carl Ostenfeld, and subsequently named by him in 1921 as variety *flavescens*.

Fifty years later, in 1970, the Belgian botanist D. Geerinck published the first full review of the naming of the kangaroo paws. He did not describe any new species, but followed Mueller's 1873 proposal that *Macropidia* should not remain separated from *Anigozanthos* as a distinct genus. He also argued that *A. viridis* should be regarded merely as a variety of *A. bicolor*, and reinstated Domin's *A. gabrieliae* as a species in its own right. Only this last argument is supported by current Australian opinion.

In 1974, Alex George of the Western Australian Herbarium named the branched catspaw *Anigozanthos onycis*. He first saw the species in 1962, when specimens appeared at a flower show at Kalgoorlie, several hundred kilometres inland from the nearest known population of kangaroo paws or catspaws. The source of the flowers could not be traced. Seven years later, however, new specimens were collected from a farm near South Stirling, north-east of Albany, and brought to the Herbarium by Mrs Honor Venning, an active member of the Western Australian Wildflower Society. Another collection from the same area in 1972 by Bob Dixon (now Horticultural Advisor at Kings Park and Botanic Garden) was used by George to formally name the species as new in 1974.

Alex George also made an important collection of an unusual catspaw north of Kalbarri in 1969. This proved to be the last of the 12 currently recognised species to be named. It was the Kalbarri catspaw, *Anigozanthos kalbarriensis*, described in 1978 by the author.

Karel Domin (1882–1953)

Detailed studies conducted by the author and colleagues in the 1970s addressed questions raised by Geerinck's 1970 paper. These studies led to the conclusion that *Macropidia* and *Anigozanthos* should remain as distinct genera, and that *A. viridis* and *A. bicolor* should be recognised as distinct species.

Subsequently, a new classification of subgenera and sections within *Anigozanthos* was developed, and several new subspecies were described. The latter included the Mogumber catspaw *A. humilis* subsp. *chrysanthus*, the inland and southern races of *A. bicolor* (subspecies *exstans* and *decrescens*, respectively), the dwarf green kangaroo paw *A. viridis* subsp. *terraspectans*, and the northern race of *A. manglesii* (subsp. *quadrans*). One of these (*A. humilis* subsp. *chrysanthus*) was the tall, pure-yellow catspaw first described informally by James Drummond 150 years ago, and subsequently collected at Mogumber in 1898 by the German self-taught naturalist Richard Helms, who at the time was a government fruit inspector in Western Australia. This attractive but rare subspecies was not recognised as new by many botanists who examined collections by these gentlemen at Kew and in Australian herbaria.

Further research has revealed the presence of at least two as yet undescribed subspecies: the remarkable giant catspaw *A. humilis* subsp. '*grandis*', and the northernmost green kangaroo paw *A. viridis* subsp. '*metallica*'. Thus, two hundred years after Labillardière's first collection of a kangaroo paw, there are still forms of these striking plants to be identified and described.

In the meantime, the perennial argument about whether or not *Macropidia* should be regarded as a genus distinct from *Anigozanthos* has surfaced again. Independent workers from the USA and Sweden using new computer-based methods of analysis have argued against recognising two genera. However, their techniques deliberately ignore the very characteristics that traditionally have been used to identify *Macropidia* and are found in no other species of kangaroo paw (for example, the unique seed and the black and green floral coloration). Hence, acceptance of their view requires acceptance of their philosophical approach and their selective use of characteristics. It seems best to let this choice stand the test of time and scrutiny by Australian botanists before deciding to lump *Macropidia* into the genus *Anigozanthos*.

It is the nature of taxonomic botany to involve questioning and refining of the names of species, but with luck the names we now use to refer to the kangaroo paws have achieved a certain maturity and stability through the past two hundred years of discovery and naming.

From botanical science to public usage

Once botanists establish names for new species, many other people, horticulturists foremost among them, can then help to make the species better known.

This is particularly true of plants as striking and unusual as the kangaroo paws, which seized the public's imagination quite early and became very much a part of popular culture. Around 1920, for example, May Gibbs featured kangaroo paws in some of her delightful illustrations for her *Gumnut* stories about Snugglepot, Cuddlepie and other bush babies.

All too often, the painstaking scientific research and field exploration underpinning the plant names we use are forgotten or taken for granted. Yet this process of naming is pivotal for the recognition and use of plants in diverse activities.

We owe a great debt to the intrepid pioneering botanists who first brought each plant species to the attention of the world by giving it a name.

Further reading

Anderberg, A.A. and Eldenas, P. (1991). A cladistic study of *Anigozanthos* and *Macropidia*. *Australian Systematic Botany* **4**, 655–664.

Barker, R.M. and Barker, W.R. (1990). Botanical contributions overlooked: the role and recognition of collectors, horticulturists, explorers and others in the early documentation of the Australian flora. In P.S. Short (ed.), *History of Systematic Botany in Australasia*, pp. 37–85. (Australian Systematic Botany Society, Melbourne.)

Erickson, R. (1969). *The Drummonds of Hawthornden*. (Lamb Paterson, Perth.)

Geerinck, D. (1970). Révision du genre *Anigozanthos* Labill. (Haemodoraceae) d'Australie). *Bulletin du Jardin Botanique National Belgique* **40**, 261–276.

George, A.S. (1974). A new species of *Anigozanthos* (Haemodoraceae) from Western Australia. *Nuytsia* **1**, 367–369.

Hall, N. (1978). *Botanists of the Eucalypts*. (CSIRO, Melbourne.)

Hall, N. (1984). *Botanists of Australian Acacias*. (CSIRO, Melbourne.)

Hasluck, A. (1955). *Portrait with Background — A Life of Georgiana Molloy*. (Oxford University Press, Melbourne.)

Hopper, S.D. (1978). A new species of *Anigozanthos* Labill. from the Murchison River sandheaths of Western Australia. *Nuytsia* **2**, 181–183.

Hopper, S.D. (1987). *Blancoa, Anigozanthos, Macropidia. Flora of Australia* **45**, 110-128.

Labillardière, J.-J. (1804). *Novae Hollandiae Plantarum Specimen*. (Reprinted 1966 by J. Cramer, Wheldon & Wesley, New York.)

Lindley, J. (1840). *A Sketch of the Vegetation of the Swan River Colony*. (Appendix to the first 23 volumes of the Botanical Register.)

Marchant, L. (1982). *France Australe: a Study of French Explorations and Attempts to Found a Penal Colony and Strategic Base in South Western Australia 1503–1826*. (Artlook Books, Perth.)

Short, P.S. (ed.) (1990). *History of Systematic Botany in Australasia*. (Australian Systematic Botany Society, Melbourne.)

The Horticulturist's Contribution

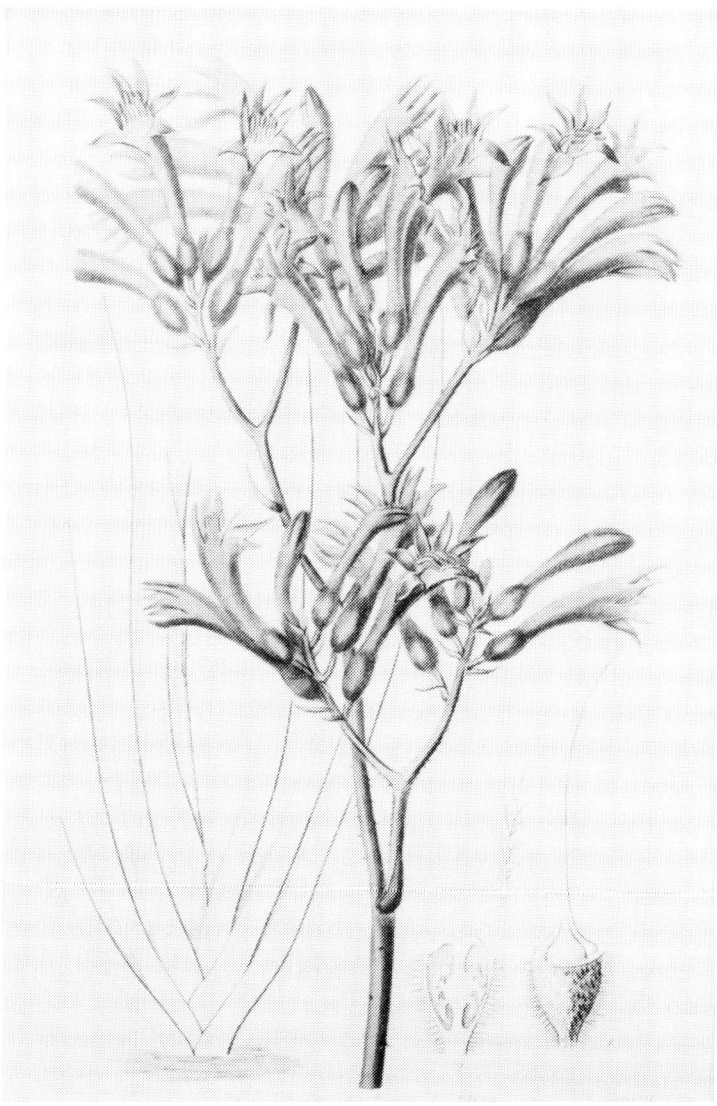

Much of the popular interest and appeal of the kangaroo paws arise from horticulturists' activities. The major period of the European discovery and naming of species last century was driven by horticultural subscribers funding collections made by James Drummond, Ludwig Preiss and others. This illustration, published in 1838 in *Edwards' Botanical Register*, is of a 'fine showy plant' of *A. flavidus* raised from seed in England by Robert Mangles. (W.R. Barker)

Cloning kangaroo paws

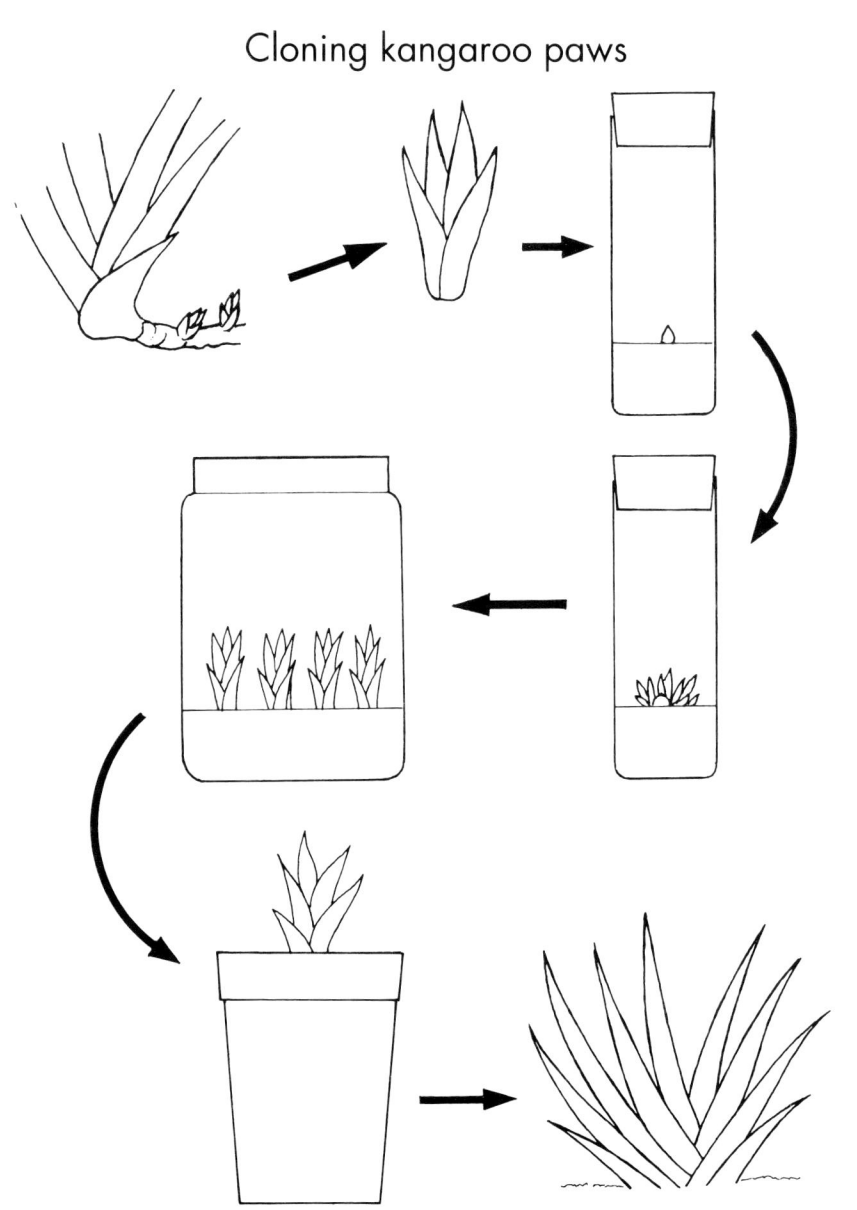

In the tissue culture of kangaroo paws, lateral buds are dissected out from the rhizome and sterilised. The tiny buds are placed in a medium containing hormones that promote shoot proliferation. The shoots are then separated and placed in a medium that promotes formation of roots. The young plantlets are placed in a pot and hardened-off under mist.

A growing reputation

Over the past decade or so, horticultural advances have made it possible to mass-produce kangaroo paws, and they have leapt from relative obscurity in the bush of south-west Australia to a position of prominence in the international flower trade.

Curiosities from the colonies

The nineteenth century was a great era of horticultural endeavour in Europe, with many a gentleman naturalist eager to obtain and cultivate exotic plants from the mysterious colonies (see Chapter 10). It is therefore little wonder that James Mangles caused such a stir in the British horticultural fraternity, with the seeds that he brought back to England from the infant Swan River Colony in 1831. The seeds produced red and green kangaroo paw plants, the colours and shape of which must have been striking and bizarre to the genteel eye of a European gardener. There are very few bird-pollinated plants close to Europe, and even the exotic rhododendrons coming to Europe from Indochina at the time, were no match for the jewels hidden in Mangles' drab seed packets. For a time they were the object of intense interest, but unfortunately European interest in austral floras waned with the passing of the nineteenth century and, for the most part, Australian science and horticulture fell into the doldrums. The fantastic kangaroo paws remained a little-known secret.

Horticultural resurgence

There was a great revival of interest in the flora of south-west WA in the late 1950s and early 1960s, exemplified by the foundation of the Western Australian Botanic Garden at Kings Park. In fact, 1960 was the year that *A. manglesii* was gazetted as the State floral emblem of Western Australia.

Although there was a resurgence of interest in the kangaroo paws, few of the wild species were suitable for cultivation. Germination of most species was unpredictable and poor, and adult plants often succumbed to fungal diseases and snail attack. Commercial development awaited some pioneering work on hybridisation initiated at the University of Western Australia by Keith Finlay in the late 1950s. In 1963 Keith Oliver commenced growing kangaroo paws to develop hybrid cultivars for the commercial nursery trade. The aim of hybridisation was to create new plants that combined the robust and evergreen foliage of *A. flavidus*, which was largely resistant to fungal disease and snail attack, with the more appealing flower colours of other species. The resultant hybrids proved quite suitable, but were mostly sterile and hence could not be propagated by seed. In these early days, the only alternative means of producing more plants was to divide the dormant rhizomes of mature plants over the summer months, and so for a time further developments were limited.

The birth of an industry

The propagation of plants was revolutionised in the 1970s with the development of tissue culture or cloning techniques, which allowed small pieces of plant tissue to be grown independently of the main body of the plant (see page 80). This enabled large numbers of small kangaroo paw plants to be propagated from minute shoot apices on the rhizome. From then on, it was possible to take a single highly sterile hybrid of horticultural merit, and culture from its rhizome hundreds of plants with identical features. Today many such hybrids are registered as cultivars and sold the world over.

It was at about the same time that cut-flower traders recognised the wealth to be found in the south-west, and the 1970s saw the start of a significant trade in wildflowers harvested from the bush. The kangaroo paws became an important part of this trade, and in 1980, a detailed study recorded the harvesting of 683 000 kangaroo paw flower stems, 39 000 rhizomes and 60 kg of seed. Most of the rhizomes came from land that was being cleared for agriculture. The most heavily picked species were *A. pulcherrimus, A. manglesii* and *A. rufus. Macropidia* was also harvested, despite its rarity in the wild, with 10 500 flower stems, 13 800 rhizomes and 0.08 kg of seed taken by pickers outside of national parks and reserves in 1980.

The next year saw the start of commercial growing of kangaroo paws to supply cut flowers to the international trade. A modest 4 500 plants were cultivated in the south-west in 1981, rising to 10 000–20 000 in the mid 1980s, and to 179 000 in 1987. By the end of the 1980s it was estimated that an astonishing 2–5 million kangaroo paw stems were available for harvesting from cultivated plants. Most of these plants came from tissue-cultured stock.

In 1991, about 2.8 million stems were exported from Australia, mainly to Japan, at an estimated value of A$1.73 million. European countries such as Germany, Switzerland and The Netherlands, as well as the USA, also imported small quantities of stems. Most exports were of red, yellow and orange-coloured hybrids, but *A. pulcherrimus* accounted for 22% of the total.

As with any fledgling industry, there have been substantial booms and busts in the commercial growing and sale of kangaroo paws. But these plants have now made their mark as an important commodity in the international cut-flower trade. Indeed, commercial cultivation of kangaroo paws is also now practised in eastern Australia, and as far afield as Israel, The Netherlands, South Africa, Zimbabwe, Colombia and California.

Kangaroo paws and catspaws in a home garden

Thus, in just over a decade, the kangaroo paws have moved from being a curiosity in the Australian native plant nursery trade, to an increasingly

sought-after commodity in international floriculture. Fortunately, there is now little need for harvesting from wild populations. Concern for the conservation of *Macropidia* led to the prohibition of commercial harvesting on public or Crown lands in 1984. Some other species are rarely taken now in the wild, because of the ease with which they can be cultivated. But species such as *A. manglesii* are still harvested in the wild in large numbers, despite the ease with which they can be grown.

Growing your own kangaroo paws

Kangaroo paw flowers make a striking spring or summer display in any garden, and some continue to flower for several months. They can be grown from seed, but without pretreatment seed germination is unpredictable, and the success rate is low in all species except *A. flavidus* and perhaps *A. manglesii*. The application of heat by means of fire or hot water often helps to induce seeds to germinate, but *Macropidia* in particular rarely germinates unless left exposed to the elements for a year or so, making it difficult to propagate it in this way. The seeds of other species usually take about 20 days to start germinating (some as long as 80 days). Seedlings can be pricked out when they are 1–2 cm high, and planted out when 5 cm high.

The easiest way to grow kangaroo paws in the garden is to obtain young plants from a native-plant nursery. Most of the commercially available stocks are robust hybrid cultivars, and there are many from which to choose.

Kangaroo paw plants grow best in sandy soils in full sun. Planting out in autumn will ensure flowers the following spring for most species. However, with irrigation, planting out can be done at any time of year, other than on very hot days. The plants respond to a little fertiliser. Mature individuals can be divided by cutting the rhizome with a knife or spade. The divided rhizome segments are then planted like bulbs directly in the soil.

Watering on the leaves often facilitates fungal attack, especially a disease known as ink spot (caused by the fungus *Alternaria alternata*), so trickle irrigation or early morning watering is preferable. Rust disease (*Puccinia haemodori*) also attacks many species and some hybrids in cultivation. Species such as *A. manglesii* are also susceptible to snail attack, and to aphid damage.

Some of the smaller species, such as *A. gabrieliae, A. onycis, A. kalbarriensis* and *A. humilis,* are very floriferous in cultivation. Their colourful compact displays are ideal for rockeries and pots. The larger species and hybrids also provide spectacular displays, and are suitable as edge plants in garden beds. The robust *A. flavidus* can form clumps 2 m in diameter, with scapes 3 m tall, so it is best placed away from edges to avoid smothering smaller plants.

A. preissii is striking, but it produces few flowers so is best planted among other wildflowers. In contrast, the floriferous species and hybrids make a bold display when planted in groups.

The possibilities are endless for selection of good colour forms of kangaroo paw species (see page 142), and for creating new hybrid cultivars. It is an exciting time to be growing these plants, and they offer the additional reward of attracting honeyeaters to your garden.

Do-it-yourself hybridising

Creating your own hybrid kangaroo paws is relatively simple, given a little patience and attention to detail. It is best done with potted plants in an enclosure or glasshouse that excludes bird pollinators. Birds will transfer pollen in all directions in your garden, and ruin your attempts to control the parentage of seed.

Fresh flowers can be hybridised by brushing their stigmas with anthers from the male parent species. Remove an anther with forceps from the chosen male flower, and rub it on the stigma of the female parent until you can see a coating of golden yellow pollen. It is advisable not to use *A. flavidus* as a female parent because it will set seed if accidentally self-pollinated. Instead, use its pollen on the stigmas of other species.

To ensure that you can trace the parentage of the cross, it should be written on a jeweller's tag, and this tied to the base of the flower just pollinated (for example, *A. humilis x manglesii*, 1.9.93).

Leave your hybridised plants in the bird-free enclosure until they have finished flowering. You will then need to wait a couple of months until the fruits mature. When they start to split on the top of the ovary(see page 97), harvest the seeds and place those from each fruit in a separate paper packet labelled with the same details as the jeweller's tag. As an extra precaution against mis-identification, place the tag in the packet with the seeds.

Hand pollination

The seeds are then ready to germinate in the autumn. With luck, by the following spring an array of colourful hybrid flowers will appear.

Further reading

Australian Plants, published by the Society for Growing Australian Plants, devoted two issues entirely to kangaroo paws: Vol. 10, No. 81, December 1979; and Vol. 16, No. 126, March 1991.

Bowden, A.G. (1991). The western star kangaroo paws. *Australian Plants* **16**, 76–87.

Burgman, M.A. and Hopper, S.D. (1982). *The Western Australian Wildflower Industry 1980-81*. Department of Fisheries and Wildlife of Western Australia Report No. **53**. (Department of Fisheries and Wildlife, Perth.)

Dixon, R. (1991). Kangaroo paw: the wild species, description, propagation and cultivation. *Australian Plants* **16**, 76–87.

Dixon, R. and Hopper, S.D. (1979). Growing kangaroo paws and related species. *Australian Plants* **10**, 199–211.

Dixon, S. and Dixon, R. (1991). Kangaroo paw plants for horticulture — forms and interspecific and intraspecific hybrids. *Australian Plants* **16**, 47–51.

Elliott, W.R. and Jones, D.L. (1982). *Encyclopaedia of Australian Plants Suitable for Cultivation*. Vol. 2. (Lothian, Melbourne.)

Ellyard, R.D. (1978). *In vitro* propagation of *Anigozanthos manglesii*, *Anigozanthos flavidus* and *Macropidia fuliginosa*. *Hort Science* **13**, 662–663.

Fang, C.S. (1983). Growing kangaroo paws: problems encountered. In *The Production and Marketing of Australian Wildflowers for Export*, pp. 164–166. (University Extension, The University of Western Australia, Perth.)

Griesbach, R.J. (1990). A fertile tetraploid *Anigozanthos* hybrid produced by *in vitro* colchicine treatment. *Hort Science* **25**, 802–803.

Hagiladi, A. (1983). The influence of temperature and daylength on growth and flower yield of *Anigozanthos manglesii* (Haemodoraceae). *Acta Hort.* **134**, 49–55.

Hopper, S.D. (1979). Hybridizing *Anigozanthos*. *Australian Plants* **10**, 211–217.

McComb, J.A. and Newton, S. (1981). Propagation of kangaroo paws using tissue culture. *Journal of Horticultural Science* **56**, 181–183.

Moody, H. (1990). Export of Australian natives as indoor pot plants. *Australian Horticulture* **88**, 38–42.

Oliver, K. (1971). New kangaroo paws. *Australian Plants* **6**, 60–64.

Oliver, K. (1991). Hybrid kangaroo paws. *Australian Plants* **16**, 52–61.

Sheperd, R.W. (1984). Selection of kangaroo paws. In *The Production and Marketing of Ornamental Plant Produce, Recent Research and Development*, pp. 57–62. (University Extension, The University of Western Australia, Perth.)

Sivasithamparam, K. (1985). Diseases. In B.B. Lamont and P.A. Watkins (eds), *Horticulture of Australian Plants*, pp. 99–102. (Dept of Agriculture, Perth.)

Tan, B.H. and McDonald, A. (1990). Pollen preservation aids kangaroo paw breeding. *Australian Horticulture* **88**(5), 49–53.

Turner, M.L. (1987). Toward the domestication of kangaroo paw. *Acta Hort.* **205**, 75–81.

Verhoogt, M.M. and Sivasithamparam, K. (1986). Ink-spot disease of 'kangaroo paws' (*Anigozanthos* Labill. and *Macropidia* Drumm. ex Harv.) in Western Australia. *Crop Research (Horticultural Research)* **26**, 49–55

Watkins, P.A. (1981). Kangaroo paws: cultivation and harvesting. *Australian Horticulture* **79**, 15–17.

Watkins, P.A. (1985). Commercial production of kangaroo paws. In B.B. Lamont and P.A. Watkins (eds), *Horticulture of Australian Plants*, pp. 92–98. (Department of Agriculture, Perth.)

Watkins, P.A. and Sheperd, R.W. (1984). Rhizome division of kangaroo paws *Anigozanthos* spp. and *Macropidia fuliginosa*. *Acta Hort.* **166**, 75–81.

Wrigley, J.W. and Fagg, M. (1979). *Australian Native Plants*. (Dai Nippon Printing Co., Hong Kong.)

Life on earth

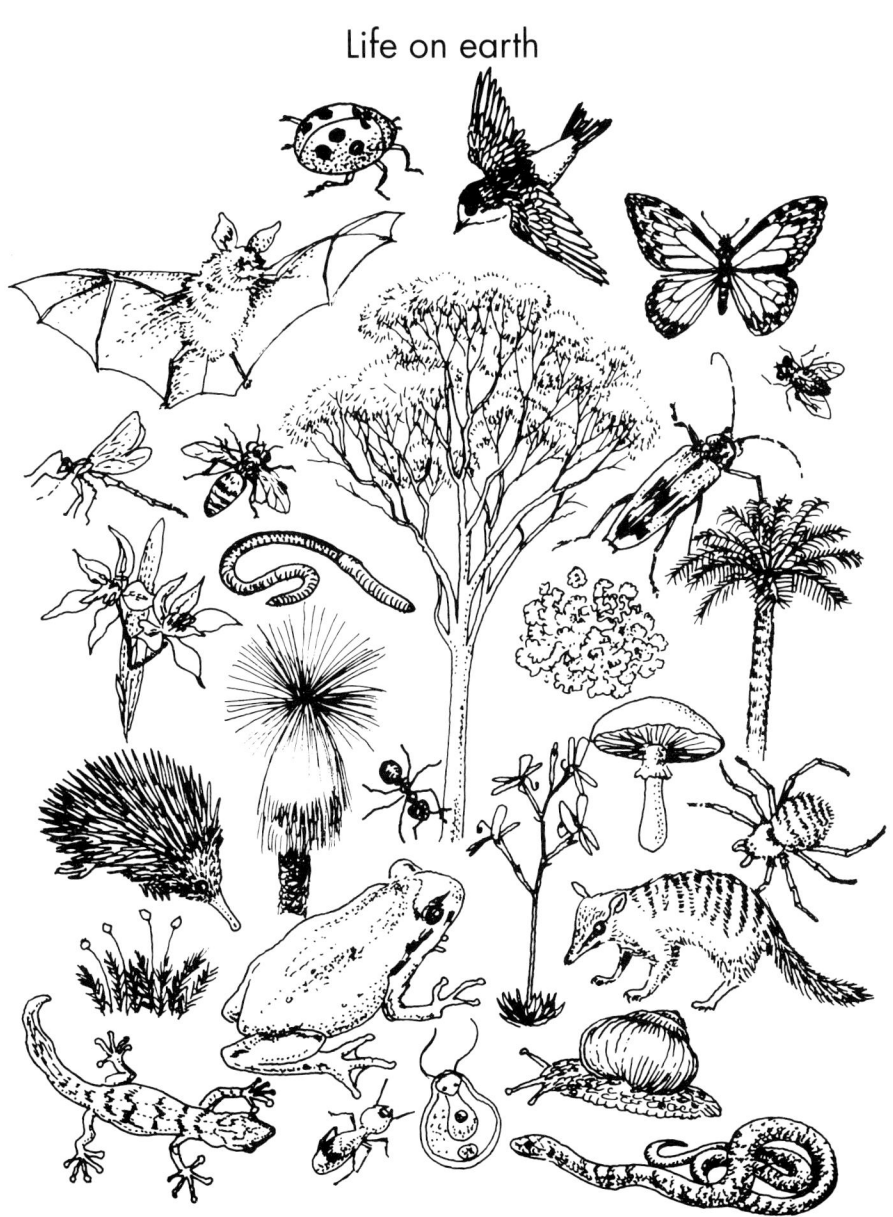

Biodiversity simply means the variety of life on earth, including the genetic variation found within species, the diversity of species themselves, and the functioning ecosystems and landscapes of which all species are part. The term 'biodiversity' embraces all the world's plants, animals and micro-organisms such as fungi, bacteria and microscopic fauna. Humans are part of this breathtaking richness.

Biodiversity: the key to our future

The conservation of the world's dwindling resources of living organisms is one of the most vital challenges facing mankind today. Like other organisms, the kangaroo paws are threatened by loss of their habitat, and of interacting animals such as pollinators. But we can act to reverse this trend.

Why conserve?

The rich and splendid tapestry of wild living organisms is under threat world-wide. Nature is dying the death of a thousand cuts as human population growth and consumption of resources increase unabated. We have witnessed the incremental loss of wild communities as western technological society has spread across the globe.

The pace of this destruction has accelerated to the point where many biologists and environmentalists are forecasting an extinction crisis like no other seen in the three-billion-year history of life on earth. Lists of endangered species are limited in their growth only because so few biologists are trained and available to document the trend.

But we know, for example, that globally a minimum of some 550 mammals, 1 100 birds, 200 reptiles, 100 amphibians, 600 fish and 2 200 insect species are endangered. In Australia alone, European colonisation has resulted in the extinction of 20 mammals and 100 flowering plants in the short space of two centuries. More than 3 000 Australian plant species are now rare or threatened, including 16% of our eucalypts. Western Australia has 43% of Australia's rare and threatened plants and vertebrates, most of which survive in highly fragmented remnant native vegetation in the south-west. Moreover, these fragments are under siege from introduced weeds, feral animals, and devastating diseases such as dieback, not to mention the ever-present bulldozer.

Fortunately, the tide of public opinion is turning on this most fundamental issue. People across the globe are recognising the seriousness and urgency of the problem of the accelerating loss of biodiversity. Policy initiatives aimed at reversing the loss are to be seen at many levels of society, from the action of farmers to protect remnant vegetation and to plant trees on their properties, to the drafting of a global biodiversity convention. In a few decades, the environment has become very much a mainstream issue in the political processes of many western countries. New concepts such as ecologically sustainable development now receive serious consideration.

Of all the vital environmental issues facing humanity — pollution, the greenhouse effect, loss of biodiversity, depletion of the ozone layer — only the loss of biodiversity is irreversible. Extinction, the death of birth, is final.

There is no second chance. Even the spectacular advances of modern genetic engineering are impotent when faced with the challenge of restoring to life the dodo, the thylacine, or Cronin's Tetratheca from the Western Australian wheatbelt. If we value biodiversity, therefore, it is imperative that endangered species are prevented from becoming extinct.

Why should we care? Because above all, every extinction is a lost opportunity. Living organisms constitute the greatest unread library available to humans. The tremendous store of genetic variation embodied in other species has already benefited humans immeasurably. We owe much of our lives to other organisms. Every breath we take links us to the plants and micro-organisms that produce oxygen. Fully half our medicines come directly from other living things. Much of our food, fibre, energy supplies and construction materials are similarly derived.

Yet we base most modern expansive agriculture on a mere handful of plants and animals, and in the process destroy vast numbers of other species with unknown potential. Future generations will require as many options as we have to deal with their world. Our short-term greed is closing off these options.

The challenge ahead is to ensure that practical and achievable methods for implementing ecologically sustainable development are found quickly. When the conservation of biodiversity becomes an integral part of the western world's thinking in ethics, economics, finance and integrated land management, the key to our future will be in hand.

Conservation strategies

It is now recognised that an integrated approach to conservation is essential, if we are to ensure the preservation of a broad range of living organisms. In the case of plants, this means both conserving them in the wild, and propagating and cultivating them in gardens.

In Western Australia, a major conservation strategy has been the creation of conservation reserves (national parks, nature reserves, marine parks etc.). These have been selected with the aim of including representative examples of all the main kinds of environments found in the State. A series of complementary smaller reserves that include sites of special significance (for example, rare communities, endangered species) has also been developed. In addition, it has been realised that other kinds of land that have not necessarily been set aside for conservation but that have remnants of native vegetation, are also a valuable resource. Examples include road and rail verges, shelterbelts on farms, and undisturbed vegetation on water reserves.

But simply setting aside conservation reserves is not sufficient to ensure their preservation. In the wheatbelt, processes such as rising saline watertables because of removal of deep-rooted perennials will affect agricultural land

and nature reserves alike, unless sympathetic management of all surrounding lands within a water catchment is undertaken. And the insidious spread of the root-rot dieback disease (*Phytophthora*) through national parks and nature reserves, especially along the south coast, is exacerbated by movement of infected soil on vehicles throughout the region. Hence, the focus of conservation strategy is now shifting towards integrated land and water management. The bush will no longer look after itself. We have to commit resources to the restoration and conservation of wild plants and animals in today's highly fragmented natural vegetation.

Endangered plants

The Western Australian Wildlife Conservation Act contains special sections aimed at the protection of endangered plant species. Once a species has been declared as endangered by the Minister for the Environment, wild-growing plants are protected throughout WA from damage or destruction by any person, unless a Ministerial permit is first obtained. The south-west has 306 plant species that are listed as endangered, the vast majority of them confined to very small sites, mainly scattered throughout the wheatbelt and Swan coastal plain.

Often, by the time a species is declared as endangered, the situation is already critical. Where extinction of a plant in the wild is imminent, there is an array of horticultural techniques that enable most species to be cultivated. Often it is sufficient simply to collect seeds from the wild and germinate them, or to grow cuttings taken from the wild. However, in some species such as *Macropidia*, the seed resists germination and more sophisticated techniques are needed. In these cases, plants can usually be propagated by culturing small pieces of the adult plant tissue. But *Macropidia* responds slowly in tissue culture, and recent research has focused on extracting the young embryos from seed, and culturing them. It would also be useful to be able to store the seeds or tissues of rare plants for future use, and the possibilities of long-term cold storage are now being investigated.

Once a threatened species has been established in cultivation, the cultivated plants can be used to restore populations in the wild, or to replenish depleted populations. This requires a sound knowledge of the breeding system and pollination of the species, so that the cultivated plants can be spaced optimally to ensure pollination and production of vigorous seedlings.

Kangaroo paw conservation

The clearance of land for agriculture, urban developments and public utilities has depleted kangaroo paw populations, but most of the kangaroo paw species are still common, widespread, and well represented in conservation reserves such as national parks and nature reserves. For example, *A. manglesii* is found in abundance in reserves such as Kalbarri, Mt Lesueur and Scott

River National Parks, in Kings Park, and in various State forests and nature reserves. It also grows on many road reserves and other remnants of native vegetation not specifically set aside as conservation reserves (see page 142).

Fortunately, these common species are resistant to the dieback disease, which is devastating banksias and other susceptible plants in remnant and reserved vegetation in the south-west.

In conserving a species, it is vital to consider all aspects of its environment. The kangaroo paws are reliant on honeyeaters for pollination, and at present these birds are common and widespread. But the extinction of several of the Hawaiian honeycreepers, which were at one time abundant, suggests that we cannot afford to be complacent.

Although most species of kangaroo paw are common, loss of habitat is undoubtedly putting the squeeze on some rare plants. There are three subspecies of kangaroo paws that are endangered, and are declared as Rare Flora under provisions of the Wildlife Conservation Act. *A. humilis* subsp. *chrysanthus* is confined to just a few kilometres of suitable terrain near the Darling Scarp. *A. viridis* subsp. *terraspectans* has a perilous existence in winter-wet swamps near Cataby, on land that is being used for mineral sand mining. *A. bicolor* subsp. *minor* occurs in very scattered populations through the heavily cleared Ravensthorpe–Esperance district. All three subspecies need close monitoring to ensure their conservation in the wild. They are being cultivated, but with some difficulty.

Variety is the spice of life

Although endangered species and subspecies demand urgent action to prevent their extinction, there is a growing realisation that conserving variation within more common species is also important. As an example, many of the widespread kangaroo paws produce rare colour forms of horticultural merit. The cultivar *A. flavidus* 'Pink Joey' is a dwarf-stemmed plant with rich pink flowers. It is now widely sold in nurseries, but all commercial stock is derived from a single parent plant. If such rarities are lost, we shall be deprived of many delightful and unusual plants.

The only way of ensuring that such valuable variants are available for future appreciation and use is to conserve large, widespread populations of the common kangaroo paw species. The most cost-effective way of achieving this is to protect remnant native vegetation in patches large enough to ensure that processes such as pollination can continue.

It is also important to realise how little we know about the potential medicinal value of extracts from the kangaroo paws. The fact that the haemocorin extracted from *Haemodorum corymbosum* has antitumour and antibacterial activity indicates that some potential exists. Conserving the kangaroo paws will enable future exploration of their hidden chemical secrets.

It would be remiss not to mention the need to conserve rare natural hybrids. Traditionally, hybrids have been regarded as the poor relations of species, and are often ignored in the development of conservation policies. This may well be due to the fact that natural hybridisation can have either deleterious or beneficial effects, depending upon the genetic compatibility of the parental species. Moreover, hybridisation is more common in some plant and simple animal groups than it is in mammals and birds (see Chapter 8). Most conservation policies have been developed with the latter, high-profile groups in mind, among which hybrids are usually aberrant and sterile (the mule being a classic case). Hybrid kangaroo paws are often of considerable horticultural interest, and can be cloned through tissue culture (see Chapter 11). Some commercially available hybrids were indeed derived in this way from solitary natural hybrids in the wild.

It is pleasing to note that a few biologists have drawn the need for conservation of natural hybrids to the attention of policy makers. Western Australia has recently changed its policy so that readily identifiable hybrids can be given special legal protection as declared Rare Flora. Some of the longer-lived kangaroo paw natural hybrids might now be protected in this way.

In the longer term, the conservation of all kangaroo paws will depend on a committed and interested public. This can be achieved through education, propagation, and ensuring that people have opportunities to appreciate kangaroo paws in the wild and in gardens. If we cannot look after such very special and spectacular plants, there is little hope for the majority of less charismatic plants under threat.

We need urgently to understand the wisdom of the many long-lasting cultures of Aboriginal people. We are part of, not separate from, the land and the living world. We must care for the diversity of life on earth, a library of unparalleled value and opportunity for us and our descendants. With conservation, there is hope for the future.

Further reading

Hobbs, R.J. (ed.) (1992). *Biodiversity in Mediterranean Ecosystems in Australia.* (Surrey Beatty and Sons, Chipping North.)

Hopper, S.D. and Coates, D.J. (1990). Conservation of genetic resources in Australia's flora and fauna. In D.A. Saunders, A.J.M. Hopkins and R.A. How (eds), *Australian Ecosystems: 200 Years of Utilization, Degradation and Restoration. Proceedings of the Ecological Society of Australia* **16**: 567–577.

Hopper, S.D., van Leeuwen, S., Brown, A.P. and Patrick, S.J. (1990). *Western Australia's Endangered Flora.* (Department of Conservation and Land Management, Perth.)

Runciman, H.V. (1989). *The Conservation Biology of Two Species of Kangaroo Paw.* MAppSc thesis (Curtin University of Technology, Perth).

Saunders, D.A., Arnold, G.W., Burbidge, A.A. and Hopkins, A.J.M. (eds) (1987). *Nature Conservation: The Role of Remnants of Native Vegetation.* (Surrey Beatty and Sons, Chipping North.)

Tan, B.H. (1989). Germination problems overcome by embryo culture in the black kangaroo paw. *Australian Horticulture* **87**(12), 46–51.

Tan, B.H. and Kan, R. (1991). Capturing the elusive kangaroo paw. *Australian Horticulture* **89**(8), 83–84.

Endangered kangaroo paws

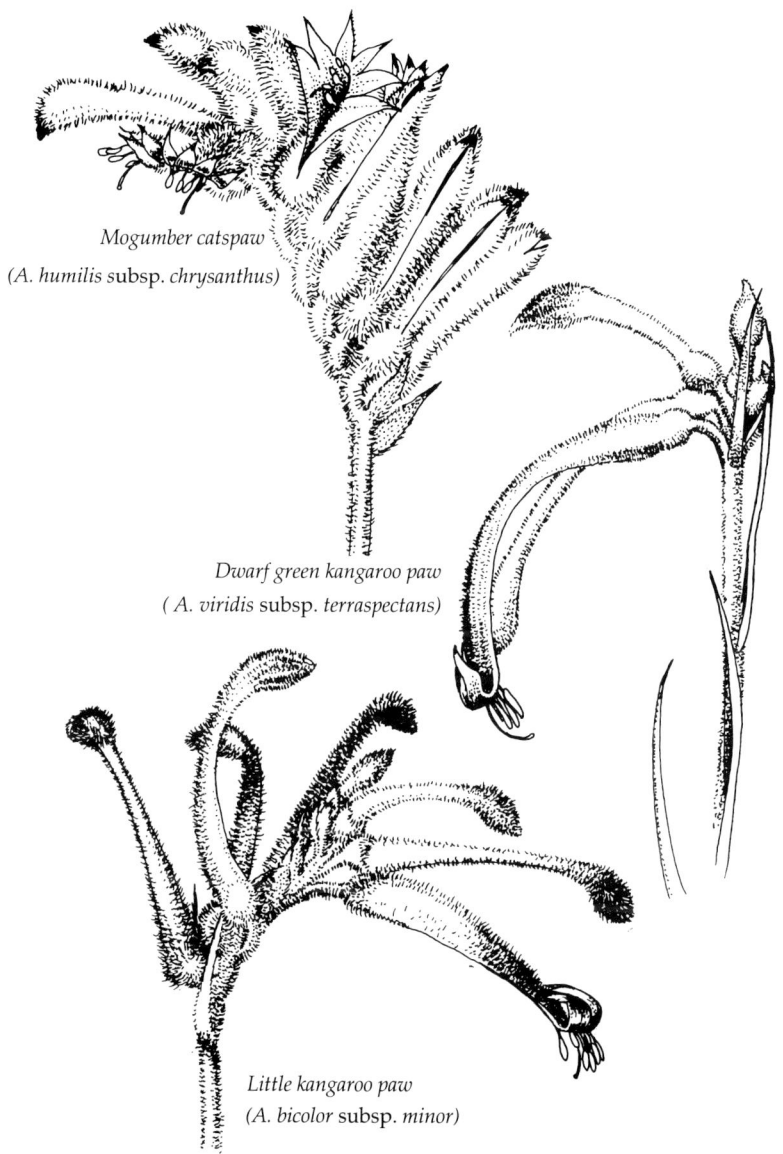

Mogumber catspaw
(*A. humilis* subsp. *chrysanthus*)

Dwarf green kangaroo paw
(*A. viridis* subsp. *terraspectans*)

Little kangaroo paw
(*A. bicolor* subsp. *minor*)

There are three subspecies of kangaroo paws that are recognised as endangered and are specially protected. Each is now confined to a very few areas, and the main threat to their survival is the loss of their habitats.

Glossary

anther: the top of the stamen, which contains the pollen.
cultivar: any cultivated form of a species or interspecific hybrid.
family: a group of genera that are botanically related.
filament: the stalk of a stamen supporting the anther.
genus: a natural group of closely related species (plural *genera*).
habitat: the environment within which a plant grows.
heathlands: plant communities that are dominated by woody shrubs less than two metres tall.
hirsute: covered with long, coarse hairs.
hybridisation: the conception of new organisms by the mating of parents that are significantly different, usually of different species.
inflorescence: the flower structure of a plant.
*kwongan***:** an Aboriginal word for the heathland and mallee heath areas of the south-west. The town of Wongan Hills is named for this term.
lobe: a pointed, projecting division of the perianth.
pedicel: the stalk of an individual flower.
perianth: the outer part of a flower consisting of fused calyx and corolla.
pollination: the transfer of pollen from anthers to stigmas, either by wind, water or animals.
rhizome: a creeping underground stem.
scape: a flowering stem.
speciation: the origin of new species.
species: a population of living organisms that is distinguished from others by recognisable features, and that can grow together with closely related species with little or no hybridisation occurring (plural *species*).
stamen: one of the male organs of a flower, which consists of a pollen-bearing anther and supporting filament or stalk.
stigma: the part of a flower that receives the pollen.
subspecies: a race of a species that is geographically or ecologically distinct from other races of the same species, and is distinguished from them by small, recognisable differences. Subspecies show extensive intergradation with other subspecies where their geographical ranges overlap or their habitats abut.
vegetative growth: the growth of leaves, rhizomes and other non-reproductive parts of a plant.
woodlands: plant communities that are dominated by trees more than two metres tall, and whose canopies do not touch.

Kangaroo paw cultivation and hybrids

1. Seeds falling from *A. manglesii* fruits. Copious production is one reasons red and green kangaroo paws are common. (Babs and Bert Wells)

2. Young *A. manglesii* seedling. The seed coat is still attached to the tip of the first seedling leaf. (Babs and Bert Wells)

3. Kangaroo paw plantlet in tissue culture. Cloning has enabled mass production of kangaroo paws for the flower trade. (S. D. Hopper)

4. Commercial cultivation of hybrid kangaroo paws. The economic usage of native plants is a powerful argument for their conservation; extinction closes off opportunities. (Babs and Bert Wells)

5. Inflorescences of *A. humilis* (left), *A. manglesii* (right) and a synthesised hybrid of the two (centre). Natural hybrids of some species are common in the wild. There are endless possibilities for creating synthesised hybrids for gardens or horticulture. (M. Lucks)

Relatives of the kangaroo paws in the family Haemodoraceae

1. Phlebocarya filifolia, *south-west Australia (S.D. Hopper)*
2. Conostylis serrulata, *south-west Australia (S.D. Hopper)*
3. Blancoa canescens, *south-west Australia (S.D. Hopper)*
4. Wachendorfia thyrsiflora, *South Africa (R. Ornduff)*
5. Barbaretta aurea, *South Africa (S. Carlquist)*
6. Lachnanthes caroliniana, *North America (S.D. Hopper)*
7. Dilatris viscosa, *South Africa (R. Ornduff)*
8. Pyrrorhiza nebliniae *South America (J.A. Steyermark)*
9. Tribonanthes australis, *south-west Australia (S.D. Hopper)*
10. Xiphidium coeruleum, *South and Central America (A.H. Gentry)*
11. Haemodorum planifolium, *eastern Australia (S.D. Hopper)*
12. Schiekia orinocoensis, *South America (G. Davidse)*

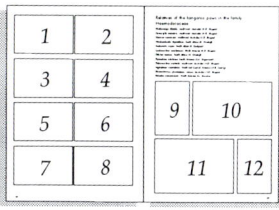

Field Guide: learning to recognise kangaroo paws

All kangaroo paws and catspaws are perennial herbs belonging to the family Haemodoraceae. They grow in the wild only in the south-west of Western Australia, where their distinctive flowers provide a breathtaking display each spring and summer. Getting to know more about our native flora can be highly rewarding, and the spread of such knowledge should help to protect these unique plants and their environment.

How to use this Field Guide

The species and subspecies are arranged in systematic order, such that close relatives are near to each other. All species are illustrated in their natural habitats, with close-up photographs of the flowers to show their structure and detail. In each case, a brief description indicates prominent features that may assist in identifying the plant, as well as its distribution, habitat and flowering season. Where two or more species are very similar, a means of identifying the species in question is provided. Any pollinators that are commonly associated with a particular species are mentioned. Where a species is successful in cultivation, some indication of growing conditions is given. These species should be available from good native-plant nurseries. Botanical terminology has been kept to a minimum, but the glossary at the back of the book may assist in understanding unfamiliar terms. A final aid for identification is the Figure illustrating opened-out perianths of all species side by side (see page 18). All photos by Babs and Bert Wells. Endangered subspecies are highlighted by a coloured border.

Opposite: Tawny-crowned honeyeater feeding on a Mangles' kangaroo paw flower (Babs and Bert Wells)

Flowers of (clockwise from top left) A. manglesii, A. viridis, A. bicolor subspp. bicolor and decrescens, M. fuliginosa, A. flavidus, A. rufus, A. pulcherrimus, A. preissii, A. onycis, A. humilis, A. kalbarriensis, A. gabrieliae (M. Lucks)

1. Red kangaroo paw *Anigozanthos rufus*

This species, the first collected and named by European botanists, has scapes 50–100 cm tall, which branch dichotomously and bear broad clusters of red flowers. The flowers are densely covered with short, matted hairs that are coloured red–purple, or (rarely) yellow. The perianths are straight, 25–35 mm long, with lobes 8.5–12.5 mm long. The leaves are 20–40 cm long, 2–6 mm wide and hairless, except at the margins, which are rough. The species occurs in seasonally wet sand in depressions. It is common in heath and open mallee from the Stirling Range east to Israelite Bay, with an outlying population at Point Culver on the edge of the Great Australian Bight. Tawny-crowned honeyeaters are important pollinators. This striking species is heavily used in horticulture. *A. rufus* is closely related to *A. pulcherrimus*, but has red flowers, narrower leaves and a more southerly distribution. Flowering mainly September–December.

2. Yellow kangaroo paw *Anigozanthos pulcherrimus*

This striking plant is common from Gingin northward to the Arrowsmith River area, extending inland up to 100 km from the coast. It is a northern relative of *A. rufus*, but has yellow flowers and broader leaves. It usually grows in low heath, in seasonally wet sand along ephemeral drainage lines and in winter-wet swamps. It grows vigorously in response to soil disturbance and summer fire. The scapes are 50–100 cm tall, branching dichotomously into numerous broad clusters of yellow flowers bearing downy yellow hairs. The perianths are 25–35 mm long, with lobes 9–13 mm long. The greyish leaves are usually hairless, 20–40 mm long and 5–15 mm wide. Eastern populations (for example, at Mogumber) have leaves that are covered with densely matted short hairs. Flowering October–December, with a synchronised peak in December.

3. Evergreen kangaroo paw *Anigozanthos flavidus*

This large, branched plant grows up to 3 m tall, and produces numerous yellow-green flowers. The tubular perianths are 30–45 mm long, and the anthers are tipped with an orange appendage. Some populations near Margaret River have predominantly brownish-red flowers (see page 142). Occasionally, plants occur with yellow, orange or pink flowers. The evergreen leaves are 35–100 cm long and 5–20 mm wide. The species is usually found in the high-rainfall forested areas of the extreme south-west, from Augusta east to Two Peoples Bay and north to Waroona. It colonises wet road verges, river banks and swamps, sometimes even growing in shallow water. New Holland honeyeaters are common pollinators. The evergreen kangaroo paw is the easiest species to germinate and cultivate. It is widely used to produce new hybrid cultivars. Flowering November–February.

4. Albany catspaw *Anigozanthos preissii*

This species is easily recognised by its large claw-like orange–yellow flowers on top of a stem with one fork. It is restricted to an area within 50 km of Albany, with an outlying population near Walpole, and occurs in low, open woodland of Albany blackbutt (*Eucalyptus staeri*). It flowers successfully after a bushfire, when it is common and abundant for one or two flowering seasons. The stem is up to 70 cm tall with reddish hairs, which are more dense at the top. The leaves are 10–25 cm long. The perianths are 50–60 mm long with red hairs at the pedicel and ovary, and orange–yellow or greenish-yellow hairs toward the lobes. The seeds are the largest of any *Anigozanthos* species, up to 2.5 mm across (see page 20). *A. preissii* also has the longest filaments (6-15mm) and the most deeply lobed perianths in the genus, suggesting that it might be the *Anigozanthos* species most closely related to *Macropidia*. Western spinebills are major pollinators. Flowering October–November.

109

5. Branched catspaw *Anigozanthos onycis*

This species is relatively rare, and is seen in abundance in the wild only after fire. It occurs in a restricted area in the extreme south of the State, from the Stirling Range east to Bremer Bay, and in the western third of Fitzgerald River National Park. In this National Park, it was recorded for the first time (in large numbers at the turn-off to Point Ann) after the devastating fire of 1989. The leaves are broadly keeled and 5–15 cm long. The branched scape is 15–30 cm tall. Flowers are dull red to cream, each perianth being straight and 40–55 mm long. The species hybridises with the common catspaw *A. humilis* subsp. *humilis*, with which it is often confused. However, *A. onycis* differs in its branching scape, somewhat larger flowers, longer staminal filaments (5–10 mm) and darker green leaves. Tawny-crowned honeyeaters are major pollinators. The widely grown cultivar *Anigozanthos* 'Dwarf Delight' is a hybrid of *A. onycis* and *A. flavidus*. Flowering mainly September–October.

6. Catspaw *Anigozanthos humilis*

This is the most common and widespread of the kangaroo paws, occurring over most of the south-west of the State, from Kalbarri south to Dunsborough and east to Hopetoun, except in heavily forested areas. The species is most conspicuous after fire, and after soil disturbance. There are three subspecies. The plants are generally small, usually only 10–30 cm tall, but the subspecies *'grandis'* may grow to 100 cm. Stems usually carry a solitary yellow–orange inflorescence. The floral hairs are yellow with varying suffusions of red or orange. Perianths are straight, and 25–50 mm long, with the margins turned down for about 75% of their length. Outer lobes are usually reflexed upwards. Stamens are paired at three distinct levels in the perianth, a feature otherwise only seen in *A. kalbarriensis*. Leaves are flat and sickle-shaped, 20 cm long and 15 mm wide. *A. humilis* occasionally hybridises with *A. manglesii, A. onycis, A. kalbarriensis A. gabrieliae* and *A. bicolor*. It is related to *A. kalbarriensis*, from which it differs most noticeably in its straight or upward facing, but never fully recurved perianth lobes. Flowering July–November.

6a. Common catspaw *Anigozanthos humilis* subsp. *humilis*

This plant is smaller than the other two subspecies, with scapes usually 10–30 cm tall, and it has more colourful orange–red and yellow flowers. Perianths are 25–50 mm long. The leaves are usually 15 cm long. It is also more widespread than the other subspecies, ranging from Kalbarri to Dunsborough and Hopetoun. It hybridises with *A. onycis*, and frequently with *A. gabrieliae*. The common catspaw is parent of many of the 'Bush Gem' and 'Southern Aurora' dwarf hybrid cultivars. Flowering July–October.

6b. Mogumber catspaw *Anigozanthos humilis* subsp. *chrysanthus*

This rare subspecies is listed on the State 'Rare Flora' schedule and is legally protected. It is confined to a small area at the foot of the Darling Scarp near Mogumber. It grows together with subsp. *humilis* to the south and west of its narrow range. It grows in sandy loam soil, in the open as well as in dense heath. The scape is 20–40 cm tall. The tubular perianths are uniformly yellow, 20–35 mm long, and relatively broad. This subspecies, although rare, is long-lived and has considerable merit for horticulture. Flowering September–October.

6c. Giant catspaw *Anigozanthos humilis* subsp. 'grandis'

This subspecies was identified by James Drummond in the 1840s, but still awaits formal naming by botanists. It seems to be confined to an area near Gingin and Cataby, and grows in rich, sandy clay loam, along creeks and near swamps in open wandoo woodland. It is instantly recognisable because of the unusually tall scapes, which are up to 100 cm long, and the large leaves, up to 24 cm long. The node of one of the larger leaves may produce a second scape. The flowers are yellow and orange, with perianths that are slightly curved, about 35 mm long, and hairy, with lobes slightly reflexed. This subspecies succumbs to rust disease very readily. Flowering October–November.

7. Kalbarri catspaw *Anigozanthos kalbarriensis*

This species is found only in the heathlands north and south of the Murchison River, particularly in Kalbarri National Park. It was named and described for the first time in 1978, and is the most recently discovered species of *Anigozanthos*. It may be seen in abundance only after fire. The leaves are blade-shaped, up to 12 cm long, and blue–green in colour. The scape is straight and 10–20 cm tall. Flowers are red, except on the perianth which may be yellow, yellow–red, or red–green. The perianths have margins that curve downwards well beyond the tube, and are 25–45 mm long, with the lobes fully recurved. The above features easily distinguish the species from nearby *A. humilis* subsp. *humilis*, with which it hybridises freely. It occasionally hybridises with *A. manglesii* subsp. *quadrans*. The species is difficult to grow in cultivation, with poor seed germination, but the floral colours are rewarding. Flowering August–September.

8. Dwarf kangaroo paw *Anigozanthos gabrieliae*

This is the smallest of the kangaroo paw species, and one of the rarest. It grows in winter-wet pink sand in depressions on the sandplains surrounding the Stirling Range. It is rarely seen because it emerges in profusion only in the first year after fire, declining rapidly in the following years. It is similar in colour to *A. bicolor* subsp. *minor*, but is smaller in flower, leaf and stem, and the flowers are narrower below the stamens. The flowers are relatively broad for their length, with the perianths 20–30 mm long. Leaves are short, being only 3–12 cm long. The scape is 5–20 cm tall. This species hybridises frequently with *A. humilis* subsp. *humilis*. Tawny-crowned honeyeaters are important pollinators. In cultivation, *A. gabrieliae* is an excellent pot or rockery plant, being very compact and floriferous. It is best grown as a biennial. Flowering September–October.

121

9. Two-coloured kangaroo paw *Anigozanthos bicolor*

This is the most variable kangaroo paw, with four subspecies recognised. Like *A. manglesii* and *A. gabrieliae*, the species has red and green flowers. It has smaller and more slender flowers than *A. manglesii*, with smaller anthers (2–6 mm long) on longer filaments (1.5–7.5 mm). It has larger flowers than *A. gabrieliae*. The leaves are flat and 5–35 cm long. It ranges from Moora, south to Nannup and Albany, and east from there to the Esperance area in isolated populations. Habitats range from open forest to low heath, usually with winter-wet soils. It hybridises freely with *A. manglesii* and *A. viridis*, occasionally with *A. humilis*, and rarely with *A. flavidus*. Flowering August–October.

9a. Two-coloured kangaroo paw *Anigozanthos bicolor* subsp. *bicolor*

The tallest of the four subspecies of *A. bicolor*, this one is easily distinguished from the others by its tall stems and robust perianths. Each plant has only a few scapes, 20–60 cm tall. The perianths are slightly constricted above the middle, 45–65 mm long. Hairs on the perianths are green, whereas those on the ovaries are red. The leaves are 10–35 cm long. This subspecies occurs on the Darling Range plateau north and south of Perth, usually in woodland, and sometimes in winter-wet clay-loam in heath. Flowering August–October.

123

9b. Long-flowered kangaroo paw *Anigozanthos bicolor* subsp. *exstans*

Short stems and elongated perianths are characteristic of this plant. It is confined to the Meckering–Pingelly area, growing in sandy clay-loam in open woodland. It grows together and hybridises extensively with subsp. *bicolor* in the York area, and with subsp. *decrescens* towards Highbury and Williams. Most plants have several scapes, some many, 10–25 cm tall. The red and green colours are clearly defined on the flower, but the perianths are pale green. Hairs on the ovary are red. The perianths are parallel-sided, or slightly constricted above the middle, and are 55–75 mm long. Leaves are only 5–15 cm long. Flowering October–November.

125

9c. Forest kangaroo paw *Anigozanthos bicolor* subsp. *decrescens*

This subspecies is distinguished by the red–purple coloration of the scapes and flowers, which barely covers the ovaries. The green perianths are 45–65 mm long and are noticeably narrowest below the stamens. The scapes are 10–45 cm tall and the leaves 10–25 cm long. It extends from Williams to Albany and Nannup, favouring swampy flats in jarrah-marri and wandoo forest. It requires more rainfall and tolerates more shade than the other subspecies. Flowering September–November.

127

128

9d. Little kangaroo paw *Anigozanthos bicolor* subsp. *minor*

One of the rarest of the kangaroo paws, this dwarf plant occurs in small populations on the southern coastal area, ranging from Ravensthorpe and Hopetoun to east of Esperance. It is listed as an endangered plant and is legally protected. Only a few of the plants have been recorded in the past decade. However, large numbers were recorded previously, after clearing and burning of mallee country for agricultural development. This subspecies is well separated geographically from the other subspecies of *A. bicolor* (see page 54). It favours well-watered sand, and has also been found near granite outcrops. The scapes are 5–20 cm tall, with leaves 5–10 cm long. The green perianths, 30–45 mm long, are strongly constricted above the middle. This subspecies has been confused with *A. gabrieliae*, but it has larger flowers and curved, not straight, perianths. Flowering August–September.

130

10. Green kangaroo paw *Anigozanthos viridis*

This species is common and usually abundant, with tall stems and eye-catching bright green flowers. The ovary and perianth are uniformly green, the perianths being 55–75 mm long, with the lobes fully recurved. The leaves are very distinctive, being rounded in cross-section, 5–50 cm long, 1–5 mm wide, and grey–green in colour. The scape is 10–100 cm tall, straight, but slightly curved near the flower head. Hairs on the stem may be red–brown. It occurs on the coastal plain and adjacent scarp, from Nambung National Park south to the Scott River and Walpole, favouring sandy depressions and locations that are waterlogged in winter. There are three subspecies. Hybrids are commonly formed with *A. manglesii* subsp. *manglesii* and *A. bicolor*. This species is often cultivated, requiring moisture and full sun. Flowering August–November.

10a. Common green kangaroo paw *Anigozanthos viridis* subsp. *viridis*

This is the tallest and most robust subspecies, with scapes 20–100 cm tall. The flowers are green or yellow–green, and they open towards the axis of the plant. The perianths are 55–75 mm long and 5–12 mm wide at the narrowest point. The leaves are 10–50 cm long. It ranges from Gingin, south to the Scott River and Walpole, always in winter-wet swampy habitats that lack a shady overstorey. Flowering September–October.

10b. Dwarf green kangaroo paw *Anigozanthos viridis* subsp. *terraspectans*

This plant is not often seen. It is declared as endangered and is legally protected. It is confined to winter-wet depressions in sandy heath near Cataby. It responds vigorously to summer fire, being a short-lived post-fire opportunist. The scapes are 10–15 cm tall and the leaves are 5–10 cm long and 2 mm wide. The flowers are green or yellow–green, similar to those of the common green kangaroo paw, but they open away from the axis of the plant. Perianths are 45–60 mm long, with the lobes fully recurved. Tawny-crowned honeyeaters are common pollinators. In cultivation it is floriferous and compact, ideal for pots and rockeries. Flowering August–October.

133

10c. Metallic green kangaroo paw *Anigozanthos viridis* subsp. 'metallica'

This subspecies occurs between Beermullah and Nambung National Park. It favours low heath and sedge in winter-wet flats and swamps. Its scapes are intermediate in height between those of subsp. *viridis* and subsp. *terraspectans* (12–40 cm tall, usually 15–30 cm). Like subsp. *viridis*, the flowers open towards the axis of the plant. Perianths are green and 50–70 mm long. It has distinctively dark metallic-green floral hairs. Leaves are 10–20 cm long. Smaller specimens of this subspecies have been confused with subsp. *terrespectans,* but the flowers overhang the recurved scape rather than being thrust outwards away from the scape. Flowering August–September.

11. Red and green kangaroo paw
Anigozanthos manglesii

This well-loved kangaroo paw is the floral emblem of the State of Western Australia. The plants are prolific and present a spectacular display. They are distinguished by the large flower heads supported by stems 30–80 cm (rarely more than 100 cm) tall. The species is common from Shark Bay to the Scott River and Mt Barker, favouring sand and gravel slopes and areas that have been burned or where the soil has been disturbed. The scape is rarely branched, and slightly curved. The perianths are 6–10 cm long, and wider than those of other species (14–21 mm). The lobes are reflexed. The floral hairs are green (rarely red) on most of the perianth, and red (rarely yellow or apricot) on the pedicel, ovary, and base of the perianth. The anthers are the longest of any species (5-12 mm). Leaves are grey–green, flat, straight, and 10–40 cm long. A rare colour form (yellow) is occasionally found in typical red and green populations. *A. manglesii* hybridises freely with *A. viridis* and *A. bicolor*. *A. manglesii* makes a superb garden plant, despite being rather susceptible to fungal diseases of the leaves. It grows best in well-drained soil in full sun or dappled shade. Flowering July–November.

11a. Mangles' kangaroo paw *Anigozanthos manglesii* subsp. *manglesii*

This subspecies is distinguished by its red floral hairs that reach only the base of the perianth tube above the ovary. The perianths are parallel-sided near the filaments. The scape is unbranched. This subspecies ranges from Gingin southwards to the Scott River and Mt Barker. It is the form seen in Kings Park and elsewhere near Perth. Habitats range from open forest to heath, where it grows in sandy soils. It hybridises freely with *A. viridis* and *A. bicolor*, and occasionally with *A. humilis*. Flowering August–November.

11b. Northern red and green kangaroo paw
Anigozanthos manglesii subsp. *quadrans*

This plant is superficially similar to Mangles' kangaroo paw, but it differs in the following respects: the scape is often once or twice branched, the perianths are slightly constricted near the filaments, the floral hairs are paler orange–red, extending further up the perianth than those of Mangles' kangaroo paw, and the margins at the base of the perianth tube are partially split and flattened to expose glossy green edges. The distribution also differs from that of Mangles' kangaroo paw, ranging from Jurien Bay, north to Kalbarri National Park and beyond to Shark Bay, where it grows in sandy soils. It occasionally hybridises with *A. humilis* and *A. kalbarriensis*. Flowering August–September.

12. Black kangaroo paw *Macropidia fuliginosa*

A spectacular plant that grows on lateritic plateau terrain, usually in low heath and low mallee, from Muchea north to Walkaway. It is uncommon, occurring in dispersed populations with individual plants widely spaced. The branched stems bear black and green flowers, and grow to more than 1 m tall. Black hairs coat both the stems and flowers. Perianths are 5–6 cm long, with tubes 12–18 mm long, and the long lobes are curled irregularly. The leaves are 20–50 cm long, hairless, blue–green in colour, and form flattened fans at the base of the plant. The black and green coloration is unusual in the Australian flora, occurring otherwise only in another Western Australian plant, *Kennedia nigricans*, and in some grevilleas. This species grows well in cultivation from tissue-cultured material, but seeds are difficult to germinate. Flowering August–December.

Further reading

Australian Plants, published by the Society for Growing Australian Plants, devoted two issues entirely to kangaroo paws: Vol. 10, No. 81, December 1979; and Vol. 16, No. 126, March 1991.

Grieve, B.J. and Marchant, N. (1963). The kangaroo paws of WA. *Australian Plants* **2**, 107–115.

Hopper, S.D. (1987). *Blancoa, Anigozanthos, Macropidia. Flora of Australia* **45**, 110–128.

The red colour-form of A. flavidus *from Margaret River (Babs and Bert Wells)*

Red and green kangaroo paws growing with pink Pimelea rosea *on a road verge south of Dunsborough. Note the lime-green colour variants in the foreground (S.D. Hopper)*

Animals associated with kangaroo paws

1. A female katydid on *A. manglesii*, tail tucked between legs to eat the protein-rich cover of a sperm bundle from a recent mating. (W. J. Bailey)

2. Red-capped parrot. Red caps are nectar thieves of kangaroo paws, whose feeding destroys flowers rather than leaving them intact and pollinated. (Babs and Bert Wells)

3. Honey possum on *A. rufus*. Although common in some parts of the south-west, the nocturnal feeding habits of honey possums on pollen and nectar have been difficult to document. (Babs and Bert Wells)

4. Male western spinebill, one of the smallest honeyeaters, which feeds on kangaroo paw nectar. It pollinates the flowers of several species, and is the major pollinator of Albany catspaws. (Babs and Bert Wells)

5. Western grey kangaroo, the largest marsupial of the south-west, after whom the name "kangaroo paw" was coined. Western greys graze on some kangaroo paw species. (Babs and Bert Wells)

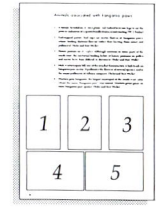

Index

Scientific names are those in current use and are indexed for the entire text; numbers in bold type refer to main entries in the Field Guide. Common names are indexed only for the Field Guide.

Scientific names

Anigozanthos
bicolor 18, 20, 22, 25, 26, 29, 30, 32, 39, 51, 54, 56, 58, 61, 63, 72, 73, 74, 75, 76, 77, 101, 113, **122**, 131, 137
bicolor subsp. *bicolor* 54, **122**, 124
bicolor subsp. *decrescens* 39, 54, **126**
bicolor subsp. *exstans* 54, **124**
bicolor subsp. *minor* 54, 61, 75, 92, 95, 120, **129**
flavidus 13, 15, 18, 20, 22, 25, 26, 29, 30, 32, 33, 36, 50, 56, 62, 65, 69, 70, 71, 72, 79, 81, 84, 85, 86, 92, 101, **106**, 111, 122, 142
gabrieliae 12, 18, 22, 25, 26, 29, 34, 50, 54, 58, 61, 76, 84, 101, 113, **120**, 122, 129
humilis 11, 12, 18, 20, 22, 25, 26, 30, 32, 38, 39, 42, 43, 48, 50, 51, 53, 56, 58, 61, 63, 70, 72, 73, 77, 84, 85, 97, 101, **113**, 122, 137, 138
humilis subsp. *'grandis'* 73, 77, **117**
humilis subsp. *chrysanthus* 13, 73, 77, 92, 95, **114**
humilis subsp. *humilis* 13, 39, 57, 73, 76, 111, **113**, 114, 118, 120
kalbarriensis 12, 18, 20, 22, 25, 26, 51, 58, 76, 84, 101, 113, **118**, 138
manglesii 8, 9, 10, 11, 12, 13, 18, 20, 21, 22, 23, 25, 26, 32, 38, 39, 43, 44, 45, 47, 48, 51, 52, 53, 56, 57, 58, 61, 63, 65, 68, 69, 70, 73, 75, 76, 77, 81, 82, 84, 85, 86, 91, 97, 101, 113, 122, 131, **137**, 142, 143
manglesii subsp. *manglesii* 56, **137**
manglesii subsp. *quadrans* 56, 77, **138**
onycis 12, 13, 18, 20, 22, 24, 25, 26, 28, 34, 35, 51, 76, 84, 101, **111**, 113
preissii 12, 18, 20, 22, 25, 26, 34, 36, 69, 72, 73, 84, 101, **108**, 143
pulcherrimus 11, 18, 19, 20, 21, 22, 25, 26, 29, 34, 36, 37, 38, 40, 45, 46, 50, 58, 61, 73, 74, 82, 101, 103, **105**
rufus 11, 18, 19, 22, 25, 26, 29, 30, 32, 34, 50, 58, 61, 65, 66, 67, 69, 75, 82, 101, **103**, 105, 143
viridis 13, 18, 20, 22, 25, 26, 32, 50, 51, 58, 61, 70, 72, 73, 76, 101, 122, **131**, 132, 137
viridis subsp. *'metallica'* 77, **134**
viridis subsp. *terraspectans* 12, 34, 57, 77, 92, 95, **132**, 134
viridis subsp. *viridis* 2, 57, **131**, 134

Macropidia
fuliginosa 10, 14, 18, 19, 20, 22, 26, 28, 36, 37, 38, 101, **140**

Common names

(Names are of kangaroo paws unless identified as catspaws)

Albany catspaw 108
black 140
branched catspaw 111
catspaw 113
common catspaw 113
common green 131
dwarf green 132
dwarf 120
evergreen 106
forest 126
giant catspaw 117
green 131
Kalbarri catspaw 118
little 129
long-flowered 124
Mangles' 137
metallic green 134
Mogumber catspaw 114
northern red and green 138
red and green 137
red 103
two-coloured 122
yellow 105